TRUTH
In Defense of the Rapture

Heather L. Rivard

© 2017 Heather L. Rivard

All rights reserved. This book or parts thereof may not be reproduced in any form, stored in any retrieval system, or transmitted in any form by any means—electronic, mechanical, photocopy, recording, or otherwise—without prior written permission of the author, except as provided by United States of America copyright law.

Cover Art provided by Jackie Church

TRUTH: IN DEFENSE OF THE PRE-TRIB RAPTURE

We are roughly 2000 years removed from the greatest miracle in the history of the world: the resurrection of Jesus Christ. As believers in Jesus, our faith is predicated upon that which we cannot see. We did not live when Jesus walked the earth. We did not hear Him minister to the masses. We did not see Him suffer before He was crucified. We did not see Him hanging on the cross. We did not witness Him laying His life down. We did not see Him buried. We did not witness His resurrection. We did not see Him alive afterward. We did not see Him ascend to heaven. However, we believe all those things happened. We also believe He will return for us one day. While there are differing opinions on the timing of His return as well as the varying implications of His return, the Bible lays out a very clear sequence of events. Much of what will occur in the end times is predicated upon the greatest miracle in history, for if Jesus did not rise, we would have no hope of resurrection. But He did, and we do. The Bible is very clear about the timing of the resurrections, as well as the people groups to which they apply. The church age is a unique period of time, as is the resurrection which relates to the church age. This resurrection is the first part of what is commonly referred to as the rapture of the church. When will this resurrection occur? That's what we're about to find out.

Table of Contents

Chapter One – The Third Day 4
Chapter Two – Every Man in His Own Order 11
Chapter Three – The Grafting in of the Gentiles 18
Chapter Four – The Word of His Patience 27
Chapter Five – Caught Up Together 32
Chapter Six – Behold I Shew You a Mystery 36
Chapter Seven – The Things That Shall Be Hereafter 40
Chapter Eight – The Seven-Sealed Scroll 51
Chapter Nine – Enoch and Noah 61
Chapter Ten – The Ancient Jewish Wedding Ceremony 69
    The Marriage Covenant and the Bride Price 72
    The Cup 74
    Gifts for the Bride 76
    Mikveh 77
    Preparing a Place 78
    A Waiting Bride Consecrated 79
    Bridegroom Comes for His Bride 81
    Seven Days in the Wedding Chamber 82
    Marriage Supper 84
Chapter Eleven – The Jewish Wedding and the First Adam 86
    The Marriage Covenant and the Bride Price 87
    The Cup 88
    Gifts for the Bride 89
    Mikveh 91
    Preparing a Place 92
    The Waiting Bride Consecrated 93
    Bridegroom Comes for His Bride 95
    Seven Days in the Wedding Chamber 96
    Marriage Supper 98
Chapter Twelve – The Divisiveness of the Pre-Trib Rapture 99
About the Author 102
References 103

Chapter One – The Third Day

It was difficult to decide where to begin writing, because there is so much I want to include. The discussion of the timing of the rapture of the church and its corresponding resurrection is only one piece in a huge puzzle. Without a framework, we are left with pieces which make less sense than they should. Thus, I have decided to start at the beginning, which is to say, all the way back in Genesis 1.

In previous books, I have written about the redemptive story and how that redemptive story incorporates each of the seven feasts of the Lord as given in Leviticus. The beginning of the redemptive story is found in Genesis 1:26-27 where God says the following:

> *Genesis 1:26 And God said, Let us make man in our image, after our likeness: and let them have dominion over the fish of the sea, and over the fowl of the air, and over the cattle, and over all the earth, and over every creeping thing that creepeth upon the earth. 27 So God created man in his own image, in the image of God created he him; male and female created he them.[1]*

Whose image and likeness was man made in? The image and likeness of our Trinitarian Creator God, which is why we are told man was made in "our image" while also being told God created man in "his own image". God is one being with a triune nature, and He stands alone as Creator. Like our Creator, we also have a triune nature. Genesis 2:7 confirms this.

> *Genesis 2:7 And the LORD God formed man of the dust of the ground, and breathed into his nostrils the breath of life; and man became a living soul.[2]*

Formed from the dust of the ground, man was given a body. Of the triune nature, Jesus is God in the flesh.

> *Hebrews 10:5 Wherefore when he cometh into the world, he saith, Sacrifice and offering thou wouldest not, but a body hast thou prepared me:[3]*
>
> *Hebrews 2:14 Forasmuch then as the children are partakers of flesh and blood, he also himself likewise took part of the same; that through death he might destroy him that had the power of death, that is, the devil; 15 And deliver them who through fear of death were all their lifetime subject to bondage.[4]*
>
> *John 1:14 And the Word was made flesh, and dwelt among us, (and we beheld his glory, the glory as of the only begotten of the Father,) full of grace and truth.[5]*

Breathed into man's nostrils was the breath of life. The Hebrew word for breath is "neshamah" which also means "spirit".[6] Of the triune nature, the Holy Spirit is the Spirit of God.

> *I Corinthians 2:10 But God hath revealed them unto us by his Spirit: for the Spirit searcheth all things, yea, the deep things of God. 11 For what man knoweth the things of a man, save the spirit of man which is in him? even so the things of God knoweth no man, but the Spirit of God.[7]*

After having been given a body and a spirit, man became a living soul. Our soul links us to our eternal destination. Of the triune nature, God the Father, who is a Spirit, is also the keeper of our souls.

> *John 4:24 God is a Spirit: and they that worship him must worship him in spirit and in truth.[8]*
>
> *Hebrews 10:38 Now the just shall live by faith: but if any man draw back, my soul shall have no pleasure in him. 39 But we are not of them who draw back unto perdition; but of them that believe to the saving of the soul.[9]*

> *John 10:25 Jesus answered them, I told you, and ye believed not: the works that I do in my Father's name, they bear witness of me. 26 But ye believe not, because ye are not of my sheep, as I said unto you. 27 My sheep hear my voice, and I know them, and they follow me: 28 And I give unto them eternal life; and they shall never perish, neither shall any man pluck them out of my hand. 29 My Father, which gave them me, is greater than all; and no man is able to pluck them out of my Father's hand. 30 I and my Father are one.*[10]

After the creation of man and woman, a perfect relationship between them and God existed. This perfect relationship came to a halt when man chose to sin willfully against God's law. Thus, sin entered the world. Genesis 2:17 and Romans 6:23 both tell us the penalty of sin is death. There has only ever been one person in the history of the world who has been able to overcome the penalty of sin: Jesus Christ.

God's redemptive plan for mankind included Him sending Himself in the person of Jesus Christ to earth to pay the ultimate penalty for all sins, past, present, and future. Since man was responsible for breaking God's law, man would have to pay the penalty of sin. However, all of mankind is born with a sin nature. Therefore, man deserves to die and would suffer justly on account of being sinful. The only man who could ever atone with finality for the sin of mankind was the man who knew no sin of His own: Jesus Christ.

> *II Corinthians 5:18 And all things are of God, who hath reconciled us to himself by Jesus Christ, and hath given to us the ministry of reconciliation; 19 To wit, that God was in Christ, reconciling the world unto himself, not imputing their trespasses unto them; and hath committed unto us the word of reconciliation. 20 Now then we are ambassadors for Christ, as though God did beseech you by us: we pray you in Christ's stead, be ye reconciled to God. 21 For he hath made him to be sin for us, who knew no sin; that we might be made the righteousness of God in him.*[11]

Having had the sin of the world laid upon His head, Jesus nailed it to the cross and laid His life down in our places.

> *Isaiah 53:4 Surely he hath borne our griefs, and carried our sorrows: yet we did esteem him stricken, smitten of God, and afflicted. 5 But he was wounded for our transgressions, he was bruised for our iniquities: the chastisement of our peace was upon him; and with his stripes we are healed. 6 All we like sheep have gone astray; we have turned every one to his own way; and the LORD hath laid on him the iniquity of us all. 7 He was oppressed, and he was afflicted, yet he opened not his mouth: he is brought as a lamb to the slaughter, and as a sheep before her shearers is dumb, so he openeth not his mouth. 8 He was taken from prison and from judgment: and who shall declare his generation? for he was cut off out of the land of the living: for the transgression of my people was he stricken. 9 And he made his grave with the wicked, and with the rich in his death; because he had done no violence, neither was any deceit in his mouth.*[12]

Jesus died as the Passover Lamb, but that is, by no means, the end of the redemptive story. Rather, the redemptive story has three parts. These three parts are what we refer to as the Gospel message.

> *I Corinthians 15:1 Moreover, brethren, I declare unto you the gospel which I preached unto you, which also ye have received, and wherein ye stand; 2 By which also ye are saved, if ye keep in memory what I preached unto you, unless ye have believed in vain. 3 For I delivered unto you first of all that which I also received, how that Christ died for our sins according to the scriptures; 4 And that he was buried, and that he rose again the third day according to the scriptures:*[13]

Before Jesus went to the cross, He foretold of His resurrection on the third day.

> *John 2:19 Jesus answered and said unto them, Destroy this temple, and in three days I will raise it up.*[14]

> *Matthew 12:38 Then certain of the scribes and of the Pharisees answered, saying, Master, we would see a sign from thee. 39 But he answered and said unto them, An evil and adulterous generation seeketh after a sign; and there shall no sign be given to it, but the sign of the prophet Jonas: 40 For as Jonas was three days and three nights in the whale's belly; so shall the Son of man be three days and three nights in the heart of the earth.*[15]

In fact, enough people were aware of His statements that they both tried to use His statements against Him and later mocked Him for them.

> *Matthew 26:59 Now the chief priests, and elders, and all the council, sought false witness against Jesus, to put him to death; 60 But found none: yea, though many false witnesses came, yet found they none. At the last came two false witnesses, 61 And said, This fellow said, I am able to destroy the temple of God, and to build it in three days. 62 And the high priest arose, and said unto him, Answerest thou nothing? what is it which these witness against thee?*[16]

> *Matthew 27:35 And they crucified him, and parted his garments, casting lots: that it might be fulfilled which was spoken by the prophet, They parted my garments among them, and upon my vesture did they cast lots. 36 And sitting down they watched him there; 37 And set up over his head his accusation written, THIS IS JESUS THE KING OF THE JEWS. 38 Then were there two thieves crucified with him, one on the right hand, and another on the left. 39 And they that passed by reviled him, wagging their heads, 40 And saying, Thou that destroyest the temple, and buildest it in three days, save thyself. If thou be the Son of God, come down from the cross. 41 Likewise also the chief priests mocking him, with the scribes and elders, said, 42 He saved others; himself he cannot save. If he be the King of Israel, let him now come down from the cross, and we will believe him.*[17]

But rise again on the third day He did, just as He said He would.

> *John 10:14 I am the good shepherd, and know my sheep, and am known of mine. 15 As the Father knoweth me, even so know I the Father: and I lay down my life for the sheep. 16 And other sheep I have, which are not of this fold: them also I must bring, and they shall hear my voice; and there shall be one fold, and one shepherd. 17 Therefore doth my Father love me, because I lay down my life, that I might take it again. 18 No man taketh it from me, but I lay it down of myself. I have power to lay it down, and I have power to take it again. This commandment have I received of my Father.* [18]

> *Matthew 28:1 In the end of the sabbath, as it began to dawn toward the first day of the week, came Mary Magdalene and the other Mary to see the sepulchre. 2 And, behold, there was a great earthquake: for the angel of the Lord descended from heaven, and came and rolled back the stone from the door, and sat upon it. 3 His countenance was like lightning, and his raiment white as snow: 4 And for fear of him the keepers did shake, and became as dead men. 5 And the angel answered and said unto the women, Fear not ye: for I know that ye seek Jesus, which was crucified. 6 He is not here: for he is risen, as he said. Come, see the place where the Lord lay.* [19]

When He rose from the grave, Jesus became the firstfruits of the dead.

> *I Corinthians 15:20 But now is Christ risen from the dead, and become the firstfruits of them that slept.* [20]

He also conquered death and hell and has all power over them.

> *Revelation 1:18 I am he that liveth, and was dead; and, behold, I am alive for evermore, Amen; and have the keys of hell and of death.* [21]

That Jesus rose from the grave and conquered death and hell is the greatest miracle in the history of the world. It is only because He rose that we have the same hope of resurrection.

> *I Corinthians 15:14 And if Christ be not risen, then is our preaching vain, and your faith is also vain. 15 Yea, and we are found false witnesses of God; because we have testified of God that he raised up Christ: whom he raised not up, if so be that the dead rise not. 16 For if the dead rise not, then is not Christ raised: 17 And if Christ be not raised, your faith is vain; ye are yet in your sins. 18 Then they also which are fallen asleep in Christ are perished. 19 If in this life only we have hope in Christ, we are of all men most miserable.[22]*

But there is still yet more to the story…

Chapter Two – Every Man in His Own Order

References to the resurrection at the end of the age are found in both the Old and New Testaments. It is necessary to understand the basic framework before we can begin looking at the timing of other events, specifically other resurrections. We will begin in I Corinthians 15.

> *I Corinthians 15:20 But now is Christ risen from the dead, and become the firstfruits of them that slept. 21 For since by man came death, by man came also the resurrection of the dead. 22 For as in Adam all die, even so in Christ shall all be made alive. 23 But every man in his own order: Christ the firstfruits; afterward they that are Christ's at his coming. 24 Then cometh the end, when he shall have delivered up the kingdom to God, even the Father; when he shall have put down all rule and all authority and power. 25 For he must reign, till he hath put all enemies under his feet. 26 The last enemy that shall be destroyed is death.*[23]

There are three resurrections detailed in the verses above. In verse 20, we are told of Jesus's resurrection on the third day, which was also the Feast of Firstfruits. In verse 23, we are told of the resurrection which will occur in conjunction with His coming. Verse 24 tells us which coming is in view, for immediately after the resurrection comes the end when He will deliver up the Kingdom to God and put down all rule and authority. This is a reference to Jesus's establishment of His Millennial Kingdom on earth which is also the end of the age. We can be sure of this from verses 25 and 26 which allude to His reign on earth. In referencing the final defeat of death, we are also given the timing of the third resurrection. Revelation 20 tells us the final defeat of death will occur at the end of Jesus's Millennial Reign. This will occur at the Great White Throne.

> *Revelation 20:7 And when the thousand years are expired, Satan shall be loosed out of his prison, 8 And shall go out to deceive the nations which are in the four quarters of the*

> *earth, Gog, and Magog, to gather them together to battle: the number of whom is as the sand of the sea. 9 And they went up on the breadth of the earth, and compassed the camp of the saints about, and the beloved city: and fire came down from God out of heaven, and devoured them. 10 And the devil that deceived them was cast into the lake of fire and brimstone, where the beast and the false prophet are, and shall be tormented day and night for ever and ever. 11 And I saw a great white throne, and him that sat on it, from whose face the earth and the heaven fled away; and there was found no place for them. 12 And I saw the dead, small and great, stand before God; and the books were opened: and another book was opened, which is the book of life: and the dead were judged out of those things which were written in the books, according to their works. 13 And the sea gave up the dead which were in it; and death and hell delivered up the dead which were in them: and they were judged every man according to their works. 14 And death and hell were cast into the lake of fire. This is the second death. 15 And whosoever was not found written in the book of life was cast into the lake of fire.*[24]

At the end of the Millennial Kingdom, death will be permanently defeated when it and hell are cast into the Lake of Fire. There will be no more resurrections after that point.

It is pertinent to back up and discuss the second resurrection listed in the verses above from I Corinthians 15, specifically verse 23 – the resurrection at the end of the age. Jesus spoke of this resurrection during His earthly ministry.

> *John 6:39 And this is the Father's will which hath sent me, that of all which he hath given me I should lose nothing, but should raise it up again at the last day. 40 And this is the will of him that sent me, that every one which seeth the Son, and believeth on him, may have everlasting life: and I will raise him up at the last day.*[25]

For the sake of clarity, we can go back to John 5 to establish the time frame for the "last day".

> *John 5:21 For as the Father raiseth up the dead, and quickeneth them; even so the Son quickeneth whom he will. 22 For the Father judgeth no man, but hath committed all judgment unto the Son: 23 That all men should honour the Son, even as they honour the Father. He that honoureth not the Son honoureth not the Father which hath sent him. 24 Verily, verily, I say unto you, He that heareth my word, and believeth on him that sent me, hath everlasting life, and shall not come into condemnation; but is passed from death unto life. 25 Verily, verily, I say unto you, The hour is coming, and now is, when the dead shall hear the voice of the Son of God: and they that hear shall live. 26 For as the Father hath life in himself; so hath he given to the Son to have life in himself; 27 And hath given him authority to execute judgment also, because he is the Son of man. 28 Marvel not at this: for the hour is coming, in the which all that are in the graves shall hear his voice, 29 And shall come forth; they that have done good, unto the resurrection of life; and they that have done evil, unto the resurrection of damnation.*[26]

In the text above, we are given both a spiritual truth and a natural truth. Jesus was telling His audience that whoever believes in Him will immediately pass from death to life. On that point, He was not referring to a natural resurrection, but to the eternal life which will be granted upon profession of faith. However, in verses 28-29, He does also refer to a natural resurrection which will occur on the day of judgment. This is the end of the age when, as I Corinthians 15:24 stated, He will return to establish His Kingdom on earth. Those who are righteous will be resurrected to enter His Kingdom and live with Him on earth for 1000 years. Similar principles of the gathering of the righteous into the Kingdom are expressed in Matthew 13 and Matthew 24.

> *Matthew 13:36 Then Jesus sent the multitude away, and went into the house: and his disciples came unto him, saying,*

> *Declare unto us the parable of the tares of the field. 37 He answered and said unto them, He that soweth the good seed is the Son of man; 38 The field is the world; the good seed are the children of the kingdom; but the tares are the children of the wicked one; 39 The enemy that sowed them is the devil; the harvest is the end of the world; and the reapers are the angels. 40 As therefore the tares are gathered and burned in the fire; so shall it be in the end of this world. 41 The Son of man shall send forth his angels, and they shall gather out of his kingdom all things that offend, and them which do iniquity; 42 And shall cast them into a furnace of fire: there shall be wailing and gnashing of teeth. 43 Then shall the righteous shine forth as the sun in the kingdom of their Father. Who hath ears to hear, let him hear.[27]*

> *Matthew 24:29 Immediately after the tribulation of those days shall the sun be darkened, and the moon shall not give her light, and the stars shall fall from heaven, and the powers of the heavens shall be shaken: 30 And then shall appear the sign of the Son of man in heaven: and then shall all the tribes of the earth mourn, and they shall see the Son of man coming in the clouds of heaven with power and great glory. 31 And he shall send his angels with a great sound of a trumpet, and they shall gather together his elect from the four winds, from one end of heaven to the other.[28]*

It is paramount to understand who Jesus's audience was at the time He spoke those words. It was not until after His death, resurrection, ascension, and the conversion of Paul in Acts 9 that the Gospel was taken to the Gentiles. The Jews had to reject it and Him first. This, they did, but John 5-6, Matthew 13, and Matthew 24 came before all of that. At the time of His words, Jesus's audience would have been entirely Jewish. Thus, the resurrection at the end of the age is one which will include the righteous Jews. Does Scripture confirm this?

> *Hosea 6:1 Come, and let us return unto the LORD: for he hath torn, and he will heal us; he hath smitten, and he will bind us up. 2 After two days will he revive us: in the third day he will raise us up, and we shall live in his sight. 3 Then shall*

> we know, if we follow on to know the LORD: his going forth is prepared as the morning; and he shall come unto us as the rain, as the latter and former rain unto the earth. 4 O Ephraim, what shall I do unto thee? O Judah, what shall I do unto thee? for your goodness is as a morning cloud, and as the early dew it goeth away.[29]

> Daniel 12:1 And at that time shall Michael stand up, the great prince which standeth for the children of thy people: and there shall be a time of trouble, such as never was since there was a nation even to that same time: and at that time thy people shall be delivered, every one that shall be found written in the book. 2 And many of them that sleep in the dust of the earth shall awake, some to everlasting life, and some to shame and everlasting contempt. 3 And they that be wise shall shine as the brightness of the firmament; and they that turn many to righteousness as the stars for ever and ever.[30]

Indeed, Scripture does confirm this. The Old Testament saints and those who died in the Lord pre-cross, like John the Baptist, will all be resurrected at the last day. Because the last day is tied to the Second Coming and the establishment of the Kingdom on earth, it is also respective to the end of Daniel's 70th Week. In fact, Daniel 12:1 specifically refers to the period of "great tribulation" that will precede the resurrection at the end of the age. Jesus uses similar language in Matthew 24 to describe the second half of the 70th Week.

> Matthew 24:15 When ye therefore shall see the abomination of desolation, spoken of by Daniel the prophet, stand in the holy place, (whoso readeth, let him understand:) 16 Then let them which be in Judaea flee into the mountains: 17 Let him which is on the housetop not come down to take any thing out of his house: 18 Neither let him which is in the field return back to take his clothes. 19 And woe unto them that are with child, and to them that give suck in those days! 20 But pray ye that your flight be not in the winter, neither on the sabbath day: 21 For then shall be great tribulation, such as was not since the beginning of the world to this time, no, nor ever

> *shall be. 22 And except those days should be shortened, there should no flesh be saved: but for the elect's sake those days shall be shortened.*[31]

Such is the importance of the resurrection at the end of the age that the gospel of Matthew previewed it.

> *Matthew 27:50 Jesus, when he had cried again with a loud voice, yielded up the ghost. 51 And, behold, the veil of the temple was rent in twain from the top to the bottom; and the earth did quake, and the rocks rent; 52 And the graves were opened; and many bodies of the saints which slept arose, 53 And came out of the graves after his resurrection, and went into the holy city, and appeared unto many.*[32]

It is important to note the Old Testament saints and those who died in the Lord pre-cross will not be the only group resurrected at the end of the age to live with Jesus in the Millennial Kingdom. Those who are martyred for their faith in Jesus during the 70th Week will also be resurrected after He returns and puts an end to sin.

> *Revelation 20:1 And I saw an angel come down from heaven, having the key of the bottomless pit and a great chain in his hand. 2 And he laid hold on the dragon, that old serpent, which is the Devil, and Satan, and bound him a thousand years, 3 And cast him into the bottomless pit, and shut him up, and set a seal upon him, that he should deceive the nations no more, till the thousand years should be fulfilled: and after that he must be loosed a little season. 4 And I saw thrones, and they sat upon them, and judgment was given unto them: and I saw the souls of them that were beheaded for the witness of Jesus, and for the word of God, and which had not worshipped the beast, neither his image, neither had received his mark upon their foreheads, or in their hands; and they lived and reigned with Christ a thousand years. 5 But the rest of the dead lived not again until the thousand years were finished. This is the first resurrection.*[33]

Before I summarize what I have covered so far, it is important to clarify a point made in the above text. Revelation 20:4-5 tells us those who died for their faith during the 70th Week will be resurrected to rule with Christ on earth during His Millennial Kingdom. We are further told no one else who died during the Week will be resurrected. This is referred to as the first resurrection.

The term "first resurrection" has caused more than a few to stumble. We plainly know this resurrection of the martyrs will not be the first resurrection ever to occur. Quite simply, this resurrection is referred to as the "first" because there are two resurrections listed in Revelation 20. The second resurrection comes after the 1000 years and is called the Great White Throne, or the second death. It is not necessary to think, nor is it accurate to think, no resurrections will occur before the resurrection of the martyrs. The "first resurrection" is exactly what it is stated to be: the resurrection of those who died for their faith during Daniel's 70th Week.

Let us now summarize each of the resurrections which have been covered to this point.

- Jesus – firstfruits of the dead, Feast of Firstfruits
- Old Testament saints and pre-cross believers – end of the age/Second Coming
- Daniel's 70th Week martyrs – after the Second Coming
- The rest of those who died during the 70th Week and the unrighteous from all ages – Great White Throne/after Jesus's Millennial Reign

There are a whole lot of people missing from those resurrections. What about all of those who have died in Christ, post-cross? What about those of us who are still alive and believe in Jesus? If it is necessary for us all to die so we can be resurrected, how will He ever be able to return? The Bible gives us the answers to each of those questions. However, before we get there, we need to understand a few doctrinal points.

Chapter Three – The Grafting in of the Gentiles

It is virtually impossible to accurately interpret the resurrections if one does not understand dispensationalism. Most believers in Jesus will be able to tell you we are not under the law anymore; we are under grace. But can they tell you why that is the case? Because Jesus died on the cross for our sins, right? That's the basic answer, and it is not wrong. However, there are a few details missing.

The law was given to Moses and the Israelites on Mount Sinai in Exodus 19-20. Paul tells us in Romans 7 the law of God is perfect, just, and holy. What was the problem then? Well, man is <u>not</u> perfect, just, and holy. Paul was also kind of enough to tell us in Romans 5:20 what the purpose of the law was – to show man how sinful he is. What does acknowledgement of sinfulness lead to? Understanding how desperately in need of a Savior we are.

> *Hebrews 8:7 For if that first covenant had been faultless, then should no place have been sought for the second. 8 For finding fault with them, he saith, Behold, the days come, saith the Lord, when I will make a new covenant with the house of Israel and with the house of Judah: 9 Not according to the covenant that I made with their fathers in the day when I took them by the hand to lead them out of the land of Egypt; because they continued not in my covenant, and I regarded them not, saith the Lord. 10 For this is the covenant that I will make with the house of Israel after those days, saith the Lord; I will put my laws into their mind, and write them in their hearts: and I will be to them a God, and they shall be to me a people: 11 And they shall not teach every man his neighbour, and every man his brother, saying, Know the Lord: for all shall know me, from the least to the greatest. 12 For I will be merciful to their unrighteousness, and their sins and their iniquities will I remember no more.*[34]

Although Hebrews was written to the Jews, it contains a terrific lesson in dispensationalism. Hebrews 10 is what I like to call "the dispensational chapter".

> *Hebrews 10:8 Above when he said, Sacrifice and offering and burnt offerings and offering for sin thou wouldest not, neither hadst pleasure therein; which are offered by the law; 9 Then said he, Lo, I come to do thy will, O God. He taketh away the first, that he may establish the second. 10 By the which will we are sanctified through the offering of the body of Jesus Christ once for all.[35]*

What was "the first" Jesus came to take away? The Old Covenant predicated upon daily sacrifices and annual atonement. What was "the second" He came to establish? The New Covenant whereby we are justified by grace through faith in the atoning sacrifice of Jesus Christ on the cross, once for all. The introduction of a new covenant means we have a dispensational change.

Before Jesus went to the cross, there were Jews and there were Gentiles. Jesus came as a Jew to redeem the natural seed of Abraham.

> *Hebrews 2:14 Forasmuch then as the children are partakers of flesh and blood, he also himself likewise took part of the same; that through death he might destroy him that had the power of death, that is, the devil; 15 And deliver them who through fear of death were all their lifetime subject to bondage. 16 For verily he took not on him the nature of angels; but he took on him the seed of Abraham. 17 Wherefore in all things it behoved him to be made like unto his brethren, that he might be a merciful and faithful high priest in things pertaining to God, to make reconciliation for the sins of the people.[36]*

However, the natural seed of Abraham rejected Jesus and demanded His crucifixion.

> *Matthew 27:21 The governor answered and said unto them, Whether of the twain will ye that I release unto you? They said, Barabbas. 22 Pilate saith unto them, What shall I do then with Jesus which is called Christ? They all say unto him,*

> *Let him be crucified. 23 And the governor said, Why, what evil hath he done? But they cried out the more, saying, Let him be crucified. 24 When Pilate saw that he could prevail nothing, but that rather a tumult was made, he took water, and washed his hands before the multitude, saying, I am innocent of the blood of this just person: see ye to it. 25 Then answered all the people, and said, His blood be on us, and on our children. 26 Then released he Barabbas unto them: and when he had scourged Jesus, he delivered him to be crucified.*[37]

Thus, for a time, God has turned His face from His chosen people in order to turn it upon another people.

> *Romans 11:7 What then? Israel hath not obtained that which he seeketh for; but the election hath obtained it, and the rest were blinded. 8 (According as it is written, God hath given them the spirit of slumber, eyes that they should not see, and ears that they should not hear;) unto this day. 9 And David saith, Let their table be made a snare, and a trap, and a stumblingblock, and a recompence unto them: 10 Let their eyes be darkened, that they may not see, and bow down their back alway. 11 I say then, Have they stumbled that they should fall? God forbid: but rather through their fall salvation is come unto the Gentiles, for to provoke them to jealousy. 12 Now if the fall of them be the riches of the world, and the diminishing of them the riches of the Gentiles; how much more their fulness?*[38]

God has not turned His back on His people, only redirected His focus for a little while… to the Gentiles.

> *Acts 15:12 Then all the multitude kept silence, and gave audience to Barnabas and Paul, declaring what miracles and wonders God had wrought among the Gentiles by them. 13 And after they had held their peace, James answered, saying, Men and brethren, hearken unto me: 14 Simeon hath declared how God at the first did visit the Gentiles, to take out of them a people for his name. 15 And to this agree the*

> *words of the prophets; as it is written, 16 After this I will return, and will build again the tabernacle of David, which is fallen down; and I will build again the ruins thereof, and I will set it up: 17 That the residue of men might seek after the Lord, and all the Gentiles, upon whom my name is called, saith the Lord, who doeth all these things. 18 Known unto God are all his works from the beginning of the world.*[39]

This period of God's focal redirection is what we refer to as "the church age". The church age is unique in that there is no elevation of Jew over Gentile, or vice versa. All who believe in Jesus Christ are co-equal. The difference now is that Gentiles have been invited to partake of the covenant promises through faith in Jesus where they had not been before His death, burial, resurrection, ascension, and the giving of the Spirit on Pentecost.

> *Ephesians 3:1 For this cause I Paul, the prisoner of Jesus Christ for you Gentiles, 2 If ye have heard of the dispensation of the grace of God which is given me to you-ward: 3 How that by revelation he made known unto me the mystery; (as I wrote afore in few words, 4 Whereby, when ye read, ye may understand my knowledge in the mystery of Christ) 5 Which in other ages was not made known unto the sons of men, as it is now revealed unto his holy apostles and prophets by the Spirit; 6 That the Gentiles should be fellowheirs, and of the same body, and partakers of his promise in Christ by the gospel: 7 Whereof I was made a minister, according to the gift of the grace of God given unto me by the effectual working of his power. 8 Unto me, who am less than the least of all saints, is this grace given, that I should preach among the Gentiles the unsearchable riches of Christ; 9 And to make all men see what is the fellowship of the mystery, which from the beginning of the world hath been hid in God, who created all things by Jesus Christ: 10 To the intent that now unto the principalities and powers in heavenly places might be known by the church the manifold wisdom of God, 11 According to the eternal purpose which he purposed in Christ Jesus our Lord: 12 In whom we have boldness and access with confidence by the faith of him.*[40]

Abraham was promised seed that would number as the sands of the seas and as the stars of sky. That promise was passed to Isaac and on through the line of Jacob and the twelve tribes. However, the heavenly promises Abraham also received are not for the natural seed but for the spiritual seed, which is through Christ.

> *Galatians 3:6 Even as Abraham believed God, and it was accounted to him for righteousness. 7 Know ye therefore that they which are of faith, the same are the children of Abraham. 8 And the scripture, foreseeing that God would justify the heathen through faith, preached before the gospel unto Abraham, saying, In thee shall all nations be blessed. 9 So then they which be of faith are blessed with faithful Abraham.[41]*

Thus, through our belief in the promised Seed, who is also called the Root, we are grafted into the heavenly promises.

> *Romans 11:16 For if the firstfruit be holy, the lump is also holy: and if the root be holy, so are the branches. 17 And if some of the branches be broken off, and thou, being a wild olive tree, wert grafted in among them, and with them partakest of the root and fatness of the olive tree; 18 Boast not against the branches. But if thou boast, thou bearest not the root, but the root thee.[42]*

And how does one partake of the Root?

> *Romans 10:13 For whosoever shall call upon the name of the Lord shall be saved.[43]*

> *John 3:16 For God so loved the world, that he gave his only begotten Son, that whosoever believeth in him should not perish, but have everlasting life.[44]*

> *Ephesians 2:8 For by grace are ye saved through faith; and that not of yourselves: it is the gift of God: 9 Not of works, lest any man should boast.[45]*

You see, Jesus did all the work on the cross. He took the sins of the world upon His own head and laid His life down.

> *Colossians 2:14 Blotting out the handwriting of ordinances that was against us, which was contrary to us, and took it out of the way, nailing it to his cross;*[46]

This is what was meant of Hebrews 10 where we are told He came to do God's will, to take away the first and to establish the second. It is for this reason we are no longer under the law. Jesus fulfilled the requirements of the law, which is to say He kept it perfectly. He took all the sins of the world upon His head – sins that have been incurred by sinful mankind breaking God's law – and paid the price for those sins: death.

> *Hebrews 9:16 For where a testament is, there must also of necessity be the death of the testator. 17 For a testament is of force after men are dead: otherwise it is of no strength at all while the testator liveth.*

> *Hebrews 9:22 And almost all things are by the law purged with blood; and without shedding of blood is no remission. 23 It was therefore necessary that the patterns of things in the heavens should be purified with these; but the heavenly things themselves with better sacrifices than these. 24 For Christ is not entered into the holy places made with hands, which are the figures of the true; but into heaven itself, now to appear in the presence of God for us: 25 Nor yet that he should offer himself often, as the high priest entereth into the holy place every year with blood of others; 26 For then must he often have suffered since the foundation of the world: but now once in the end of the world hath he appeared to put away sin by the sacrifice of himself. 27 And as it is appointed unto men once to die, but after this the judgment: 28 So Christ was once offered to bear the sins of many; and unto them that look for him shall he appear the second time without sin unto salvation.*[47]

Why was the New Covenant established upon grace? The answer to that is not as simple as saying, "because Jesus died on the cross". In Matthew 26, when Jesus was praying in the Garden of Gethsemane the night before His crucifixion, He said the following:

> *Matthew 26:39 And he went a little farther, and fell on his face, and prayed, saying, O my Father, if it be possible, let this cup pass from me: nevertheless not as I will, but as thou wilt.*[48]

The cup which was not to be passed from Jesus was the cup containing the wrath of God. It was the same divine wrath which demands death for sin. God's wrath was satisfied when the penalty for the sins of the world was paid by Jesus's death on the cross. Jesus was the innocent scapegoat for the guilty world. As long as one professes faith in Jesus, in His death, burial, and resurrection, no further payment for sin will ever be necessary. It is for this reason, Paul wrote the following in I Thessalonians 5:

> *I Thessalonians 5:9 For God hath not appointed us to wrath, but to obtain salvation by our Lord Jesus Christ, 10 Who died for us, that, whether we wake or sleep, we should live together with him.*[49]

It is also for this reason those who do <u>not</u> believe in Jesus Christ are still subject to the wrath of God, the very wrath that will be dispensed by worsening degrees during Daniel's 70th Week. In Romans 11 we learned God turned His focus from an apostate Israel to the Gentiles. The church age was born, and during this age we are saved by grace through faith. However, we are told God's eyes will be turned back to Israel, specifically after the Battle of Gog and Magog.

> *Ezekiel 39:21 And I will set my glory among the heathen, and all the heathen shall see my judgment that I have executed, and my hand that I have laid upon them. 22 So the house of Israel shall know that I am the LORD their God from that day and forward. 23 And the heathen shall know that the house of Israel went into captivity for their iniquity: because they*

> *trespassed against me, therefore hid I my face from them, and gave them into the hand of their enemies: so fell they all by the sword. 24 According to their uncleanness and according to their transgressions have I done unto them, and hid my face from them. 25 Therefore thus saith the Lord GOD; Now will I bring again the captivity of Jacob, and have mercy upon the whole house of Israel, and will be jealous for my holy name; 26 After that they have borne their shame, and all their trespasses whereby they have trespassed against me, when they dwelt safely in their land, and none made them afraid. 27 When I have brought them again from the people, and gathered them out of their enemies' lands, and am sanctified in them in the sight of many nations; 28 Then shall they know that I am the LORD their God, which caused them to be led into captivity among the heathen: but I have gathered them unto their own land, and have left none of them any more there. 29 Neither will I hide my face any more from them: for I have poured out my spirit upon the house of Israel, saith the Lord GOD.*[50]

We have already learned there is no distinction between Jew and Gentile within the body of Christ during this church age. However, the final seven years of human history will once again be Israel-centric.

> *Daniel 9:24 Seventy weeks are determined upon thy people and upon thy holy city, to finish the transgression, and to make an end of sins, and to make reconciliation for iniquity, and to bring in everlasting righteousness, and to seal up the vision and prophecy, and to anoint the most Holy.*[51]

During the 70 Weeks, there was and will most certainly be a distinction between the Jews and Gentiles. The first 69 Weeks occurred pre-cross, and they were Israel-centric. The church did yet exist. Similarly, the final Week of years will send the Gentiles to the background and return the Jews to the forefront. This is opposed to what we know about the church age's co-equality of Jews and Gentiles, and it necessitates a change in dispensations. Paul writes of this change in Romans 11.

> *Romans 11:25 For I would not, brethren, that ye should be ignorant of this mystery, lest ye should be wise in your own conceits; that blindness in part is happened to Israel, until the fulness of the Gentiles be come in.*[52]

For God to shift His focus back to Israel, considering the church and Israel are separate entities and He deals with one at a time, those who have believed in Jesus Christ will need to be removed. These are those whose sins have been covered by the blood of Jesus, those for whom God's wrath has already been satisfied.

Chapter Four – The Word of His Patience

One of the most significant points of opposition to the doctrine of dispensationalism coincides with use of the word "tribulation". Many of those who do not believe in the pre-trib rapture of the church would argue Jesus said we would all have tribulation, so we need not think we will be spared from the specific period termed "the Tribulation". On the first point, I would agree. Jesus did plainly say we would all experience tribulation.

> *John 16:33 These things I have spoken unto you, that in me ye might have peace. In the world ye shall have tribulation: but be of good cheer; I have overcome the world.*[53]

Jesus further expounds upon why we would experience tribulation.

> *John 15:18 If the world hate you, ye know that it hated me before it hated you. 19 If ye were of the world, the world would love his own: but because ye are not of the world, but I have chosen you out of the world, therefore the world hateth you. 20 Remember the word that I said unto you, The servant is not greater than his lord. If they have persecuted me, they will also persecute you; if they have kept my saying, they will keep yours also. 21 But all these things will they do unto you for my name's sake, because they know not him that sent me. 22 If I had not come and spoken unto them, they had not had sin: but now they have no cloak for their sin. 23 He that hateth me hateth my Father also.*[54]

The world will hate and persecute us because of its feelings toward Him. Just as Jesus was rejected, we will be too. It is not because of ourselves they hate us, but because of whom we represent. However, on the second point, I would simply say this - the Bible does <u>not</u> say anywhere the saints who have already passed away, those who may not have been harshly persecuted in their time during the church age, will be resurrected to go through the final seven years of world history. It does not even remotely allude to such a thing. Thus, it is faulty to argue that because some church saints endured severe persecution and tribulation, we who are alive in this time and place must automatically go through "the Tribulation". More to the point, the Bible never actually calls those final seven years "the Tribulation". This is a term we have adopted for reasons unbeknownst to me. The Bible calls this final seven years of human history by other names which include Daniel's 70th Week, the Time of Jacob's Trouble, and the hour of temptation. Two of those names relate solely to the Jews. For reasons I have already specified, that should come as no surprise. However, it is important to make the distinction between "tribulation" and "the hour of temptation".

"Tribulation" is the Greek word "thlipsin" which means "persecution, affliction, distress"; properly, *pressure* (what constricts or rubs together), used of a narrow place that "hems someone in"; *tribulation*, especially *internal pressure* that causes someone to feel confined (restricted, "without options")".[55] Tribulation, as previously stated, is not what any believers in Christ are being kept from. The hour of temptation is, however, what believers in Christ were promised to be kept from.

> *Revelation 3:10 Because thou hast kept the word of my patience, I also will keep thee from the hour of temptation, which shall come upon all the world, to try them that dwell upon the earth.*[56]

"Temptation" is the Greek word "pierasmou" which means "trial, probation, testing".[57] The time period believers were promised to be spared from is exactly as it reads, a period of testing. What is the test? To choose Jesus Christ or not to choose Jesus Christ; that is the question. Will they or won't they? Because the end of the period of testing results in Him coming back and doing two things: destroying everyone who has rejected Him and ushering those who have accepted Him into His Millennial Kingdom. There are no other options. And make no mistake, everyone who goes into the 70th Week will wind up deciding for or against Jesus Christ.

Why would we believers be spared from such a time of testing? Because we have already made our decision for Christ and have no need to be tested in that manner. We have already made the decision the rest of the world has not made but will be forced to make in the very near future. Thus, based on the nature of our faith and acceptance of Jesus Christ, we have no need to remain here while the wrath of God is dispensed on unbelievers. It must be understood, that is exactly what the wrath of God is designed to do: force people to decide for or against Him and judge those who have decided against.

Daniel's 70th Week is not an arbitrary time where God will be judging people and dispensing wrath for random reasons and on random people. It is a very specific time designed with a very specific outcome. From the foundation of the world, it was always set to occur at a fixed time. It is not being delayed, we just haven't quite gotten to it yet. It is, however, very quickly approaching.

> *II Peter 3:3 Knowing this first, that there shall come in the last days scoffers, walking after their own lusts, 4 And saying, Where is the promise of his coming? for since the fathers fell asleep, all things continue as they were from the beginning of the creation. 5 For this they willingly are ignorant of, that by the word of God the heavens were of old, and the earth standing out of the water and in the water: 6 Whereby the world that then was, being overflowed with water, perished: 7 But the heavens and the earth, which are now, by the same word are kept in store, reserved unto fire against the day of judgment and perdition of ungodly men. 8 But, beloved, be not ignorant of this one thing, that one day is with the Lord as a thousand years, and a thousand years as one day. 9 The Lord is not slack concerning his promise, as some men count slackness; but is longsuffering to us-ward, not willing that any should perish, but that all should come to repentance.*[58]

There are two passages of Scripture many people link to the rapture of the church, but they do not actually regard it. They regard the assembling of Jews and Gentiles together for the purpose of teaching the gospel of the dispensation of grace prior to the end of the church age. Not coincidentally, the passages are tied together via use of one Greek word which appears only twice in the New Testament. The location of the first passage is perhaps less familiar to most, and it appears in "the dispensational chapter" of Hebrews 10. Because two of the three names I mentioned above which relate to final seven years are Jewish in nature – Daniel's 70th Week and the Time of Jacob's Trouble – I decided to start with the passage written to the Jewish people.

> *Hebrews 10:25 Not forsaking the assembling of ourselves together, as the manner of some is; but exhorting one another: and so much the more, as ye see the day approaching. 26 For if we sin wilfully after that we have received the knowledge of the truth, there remaineth no more sacrifice for sins, 27 But a certain fearful looking for of judgment and fiery indignation, which shall devour the adversaries. 28 He that despised Moses' law died without mercy under two or three witnesses: 29 Of how much sorer punishment, suppose ye, shall he be thought worthy, who hath trodden under foot the Son of God, and hath counted the blood of the covenant, wherewith he was sanctified, an unholy thing, and hath done despite unto the Spirit of grace? 30 For we know him that hath said, Vengeance belongeth unto me, I will recompense, saith the Lord. And again, The Lord shall judge his people. 31 It is a fearful thing to fall into the hands of the living God.[59]*

The verses above deal with those who reject Jesus Christ. If the Jews thought judgment under the law was bad for those who rejected God or broke His law in the Old Testament, how much worse off will they be for rejecting His Messiah, especially considering they were given the very law which prophesied of His coming?

> *John 5:43 I am come in my Father's name, and ye receive me not: if another shall come in his own name, him ye will receive. 44 How can ye believe, which receive honour one of another, and seek not the honour that cometh from God only? 45 Do not think that I will accuse you to the Father: there is one that accuseth you, even Moses, in whom ye trust. 46 For had ye believed Moses, ye would have believed me;*

> *for he wrote of me. 47 But if ye believe not his writings, how shall ye believe my words?*[60]

Romans 11 referred to the Gentiles as having the job of provoking the Jews to jealousy. After all, we have a better relationship with their God than they do by virtue of the fact we have not rejected His Messiah. However, Hebrews 10 plainly states there is no other sacrifice they can offer which will save them. If they reject Jesus, they reject redemption. No blood of bulls or goats can do that. Furthermore, due to the nature of their rejection, they currently have an adversarial relationship with God. Conversely, those of us who are in Christ have peace with God.

> *Romans 5:1 Therefore being justified by faith, we have peace with God through our Lord Jesus Christ: 2 By whom also we have access by faith into this grace wherein we stand, and rejoice in hope of the glory of God.*[61]

The adversarial relationship will bring upon them God's judgment and fiery indignation. And as Hebrews 10:31 states, it is a fearful thing to fall into the hands of the living God.

In Hebrews 10:25, the Greek word for "assembling" is "episunagógé".[62] It is used only two times in the New Testament, the other of which is in II Thessalonians 2:1.

> *II Thessalonians 2:1 Now we beseech you, brethren, by the coming of our Lord Jesus Christ, and by our **gathering together** unto him, 2 That ye be not soon shaken in mind, or be troubled, neither by spirit, nor by word, nor by letter as from us, as that the day of Christ is at hand.*[63]

II Thessalonians 2:1 and Hebrews 10:25 regard the admonition given to both Jews and Gentiles to assemble together so the gospel can be heard among as many as possible before the rapture of the church occurs. Those who have not believed at that point will be left behind.

Chapter Five – Caught Up Together

The first relevant reference Paul made in I Thessalonians to the coming of the Lord is found in chapter 3.

> *I Thessalonians 3:13 To the end he may stablish your hearts unblameable in holiness before God, even our Father, at the coming of our Lord Jesus Christ <u>with all his saints</u>.*[64]

Paul is using language from the Old Testament prophet Zechariah to describe the event which will see the Lord return with His saints:

> *Zechariah 14:4 And his feet shall stand in that day upon the mount of Olives, which is before Jerusalem on the east, and the mount of Olives shall cleave in the midst thereof toward the east and toward the west, and there shall be a very great valley; and half of the mountain shall remove toward the north, and half of it toward the south. 5 And ye shall flee to the valley of the mountains; for the valley of the mountains shall reach unto Azal: yea, ye shall flee, like as ye fled from before the earthquake in the days of Uzziah king of Judah: and the LORD my God shall come, <u>and all the saints with thee</u>.*[65]

At the Second Coming, to which Zechariah 14 applies, Jesus will return with His saints. I Thessalonians 4 also references the same event.

> *I Thessalonians 4:13 But I would not have you to be ignorant, brethren, concerning them which are asleep, that ye sorrow not, even as others which have no hope. 14 For if we believe that Jesus died and rose again, even so them also which sleep in Jesus will God bring with him. 15 For this we say unto you by the word of the Lord, that we which are alive and remain unto the coming of the Lord shall not prevent them which are asleep. 16 For the Lord himself shall descend from heaven with a shout, with the voice of the archangel, and with the trump of God: and the dead in Christ shall rise*

> *first: 17 Then we which are alive and remain shall be caught up together with them in the clouds, to meet the Lord in the air: and so shall we ever be with the Lord. 18 Wherefore comfort one another with these words.*[66]

Jesus's coming with all "His" saints is a reference to those who have died in Christ. These would be the group of deceased church saints which were missing from the previous resurrections. Paul is writing to reassure the Thessalonians that all those who have passed away will by no means miss out on a resurrection. In fact, in the sequence of events given, their resurrection comes first. Then, the group of us who are alive at the Lord's coming will be caught up with the newly resurrected to meet Jesus in the air. And so shall we ever be with the Lord. Paul further tells the church to comfort one another with these words. Those who don't believe in Jesus would have no basis for believing they would ever see their loved ones again. We know differently.

In this context, the rapture of the church is the facilitating event which relocates believers in Jesus from earth to heaven so that they can return with Him at His Second Coming. Thus, the prophecy is given with direct correlation to Zechariah 14.

In the next chapter, Paul gives the Thessalonians a brief synopsis of what will occur after the rapture of the church. They have no need that he writes to them regarding the specific details, but he gives them a basic framework.

> *I Thessalonians 5:1 But of the times and the seasons, brethren, ye have no need that I write unto you. 2 For yourselves know perfectly that the day of the Lord so cometh as a thief in the night. 3 For when they shall say, Peace and safety; then sudden destruction cometh upon them, as travail upon a woman with child; and they shall not escape. 4 But ye, brethren, are not in darkness, that that day should overtake you as a thief. 5 Ye are all the children of light, and the children of the day: we are not of the night, nor of darkness.*[67]

The "times and seasons" is a reference to the chronology of time and events which will lead to a specific appointed time. Simply put, it is a reference to Daniel's 70th Week at the end of which Jesus will return at the Second Coming.

The thief in the night has no bearing on either the church or the rapture of the church. It is solely a reference to those who will remain spiritually dark at the Second Coming. Below are two additional references which support this point.

> *II Peter 3:10 But the day of the Lord will come as a thief in the night; in the which the heavens shall pass away with a great noise, and the elements shall melt with fervent heat, the earth also and the works that are therein shall be burned up.*[68]

> *Revelation 16:12 And the sixth angel poured out his vial upon the great river Euphrates; and the water thereof was dried up, that the way of the kings of the east might be prepared. 13 And I saw three unclean spirits like frogs come out of the mouth of the dragon, and out of the mouth of the beast, and out of the mouth of the false prophet. 14 For they are the spirits of devils, working miracles, which go forth unto the kings of the earth and of the whole world, to gather them to the battle of that great day of God Almighty. 15 Behold, I come as a thief. Blessed is he that watcheth, and keepeth his garments, lest he walk naked, and they see his shame. 16 And he gathered them together into a place called in the Hebrew tongue Armageddon. 17 And the seventh angel poured out his vial into the air; and there came a great voice out of the temple of heaven, from the throne, saying, It is done.*[69]

I Thessalonians 5:3 is a reference to the event which will start Daniel's 70th Week: the confirmation of the Antichrist's covenant with the many. Daniel's 70th Week is likened to travail upon a woman with child, travail which will result in the birth of a child... or, in this case, with the return of the Messiah.

> *For when **they** shall say, Peace and safety; then sudden destruction cometh upon **them**, as travail upon a woman with child; and **they** shall not escape.*

Did you notice the three references above which infer the church will be absent? Paul knew even if the events were to occur in his lifetime, he would not be present on earth for them, nor would any other believers in Jesus. This is in keeping with the promise Jesus made in Revelation 3:10.

> *Revelation 3:10 Because thou hast kept the word of my patience, I also will keep thee from the hour of temptation, which shall come upon all the world, to try them that dwell upon the earth.*[70]

We will not be kept on earth and simply preserved through the events of the 70th Week. Our promise was to be removed from them altogether, which is why I Thessalonians 4 and its corresponding resurrection and rapture comes before I Thessalonians 5 and the events of the 70th Week. We must be removed first.

> *Daniel 9:27 And he shall confirm the covenant with many for one week: and in the midst of the week he shall cause the sacrifice and the oblation to cease, and for the overspreading of abominations he shall make it desolate, even until the consummation, and that determined shall be poured upon the desolate.*[71]

As is always the case with the concept of "two or three witnesses", there is another passage in Scripture which affirms the events of the resurrection of the church saints and the corresponding rapture.

Chapter Six – Behold I Shew You a Mystery

We have already visited select verses from I Corinthians 15 which detailed certain resurrections. Those resurrections were that of Jesus, the end of the age, and the Great White Throne. However, there is another resurrection contained within the chapter. This one is a bit of a "mystery", meaning it is something that had not previously been revealed. However, before telling us about this mystery, Paul sets the stage for its necessity.

> *I Corinthians 15:21 For since by man came death, by man came also the resurrection of the dead. 22 For as in Adam all die, even so in Christ shall all be made alive.*
>
> *I Corinthians 15:42 So also is the resurrection of the dead. It is sown in corruption; it is raised in incorruption: 43 It is sown in dishonour; it is raised in glory: it is sown in weakness; it is raised in power: 44 It is sown a natural body; it is raised a spiritual body. There is a natural body, and there is a spiritual body. 45 And so it is written, The first man Adam was made a living soul; the last Adam was made a quickening spirit. 46 Howbeit that was not first which is spiritual, but that which is natural; and afterward that which is spiritual. 47 The first man is of the earth, earthy; the second man is the Lord from heaven. 48 As is the earthy, such are they also that are earthy: and as is the heavenly, such are they also that are heavenly. 49 And as we have borne the image of the earthy, we shall also bear the image of the heavenly. 50 Now this I say, brethren, that flesh and blood cannot inherit the kingdom of God; neither doth corruption inherit incorruption.*[72]

It all boils down to the verse 50. Corrupt, sinful flesh and blood cannot be in the presence of a holy God. Thus, for us to enter the presence of God, we must first be changed. But this situation does not apply to all church saints. At least not technically. II Corinthians 5 provides a caveat.

> *II Corinthians 5:8 We are confident, I say, and willing rather to be absent from the body, and to be present with the Lord.*[73]

We know those who have died in Christ are currently in heaven and in the presence of God, just not in flesh and blood bodies. They will, however, be changed to glorified bodies in the rapture. If it was necessary that we all die in order that we might be resurrected, Jesus would be infinitely delayed. Fortunately for mankind, God does not work like that.

From the foundation of the earth, the end has been established. Human history was only ever designed to last for a preset amount of time. Thus, each event which precedes that preset time must also have been scheduled in advance. If the Second Coming has an appointed time, and we can rest assured that it very much does, then Daniel's 70th Week also has a preset time. The rapture of the church must then also have a preset time. Thus, when the time for the rapture has been reached, those who are alive in Christ need not be resurrected. All they need is to be changed.

> *I Corinthians 15:51 Behold, I shew you a mystery; We shall not all sleep, but we shall all be changed, 52 In a moment, in the twinkling of an eye, at the last trump: for the trumpet shall sound, and the dead shall be raised incorruptible, and we shall be changed. 53 For this corruptible must put on incorruption, and this mortal must put on immortality. 54 So when this corruptible shall have put on incorruption, and this mortal shall have put on immortality, then shall be brought to pass the saying that is written, Death is swallowed up in victory. 55 O death, where is thy sting? O grave, where is thy victory?*[74]

For the live members of the church to be taken to heaven, we must be changed into immortal, incorruptible forms. This will occur at the rapture of the church. Such a change is necessary for Jesus to fulfill His promise to take us to the Father's house.

> *John 14:1 Let not your heart be troubled: ye believe in God, believe also in me. 2 In my Father's house are many*

> *mansions: if it were not so, I would have told you. I go to prepare a place for you. 3 And if I go and prepare a place for you, I will come again, and receive you unto myself; that where I am, there ye may be also.*[75]

There are those who say Jesus was referring to His Second Coming, and since the words were spoken while He was on earth, He never intended to take us to heaven. They say He will catch us up at the Second Coming, change us, then immediately return to earth with us. Fortunately for us, that is not the case. A link can be drawn to I Thessalonians 4:17 which says – *so shall we ever be with the Lord*. That means whether He is in heaven or on earth, we will need the ability to be with Him. Jesus will most assuredly be in heaven for the proceeding seven years which constitute Daniel's 70th Week. Thus, we must be changed so we may not only be with Him, but so we may also be in the presence of the Father. Bible prophecy must be kept intact.

Back in I Thessalonians 4, we were told the Lord Himself will descend from heaven with a shout (to wake the dead), with the voice of the archangel (giving ultimate authority to His command), and with the trump of God (the voice of God). The trump of God was first used to call the Israelites to assembly at Mount Sinai to receive the law.

> *Exodus 19:11 And be ready against the third day: for the third day the* LORD *will come down in the sight of all the people upon mount Sinai. 12 And thou shalt set bounds unto the people round about, saying, Take heed to yourselves, that ye go not up into the mount, or touch the border of it: whosoever toucheth the mount shall be surely put to death: 13 There shall not an hand touch it, but he shall surely be stoned, or shot through; whether it be beast or man, it shall not live: when the trumpet soundeth long, they shall come up to the mount. 14 And Moses went down from the mount unto the people, and sanctified the people; and they washed their clothes. 15 And he said unto the people, Be ready against the third day: come not at your wives. 16 And it came to pass on the third day in the morning, that there were thunders and*

> *lightnings, and a thick cloud upon the mount, and the voice of the trumpet exceeding loud; so that all the people that was in the camp trembled. 17 And Moses brought forth the people out of the camp to meet with God; and they stood at the nether part of the mount. 18 And mount Sinai was altogether on a smoke, because the LORD descended upon it in fire: and the smoke thereof ascended as the smoke of a furnace, and the whole mount quaked greatly. 19 And when the voice of the trumpet sounded long, and waxed louder and louder, Moses spake, and God answered him by a voice.*[76]

The next time the trump of God is used will be to call the church to assembly in the air. This is also the meaning of the last trump, as referenced in I Corinthians 15:52. It is unfortunate some people try to link the last trump to the 7th Trumpet judgment of Revelation. We will discuss in a bit how that link cannot be accurate. However, I also find it unfortunate many people link the "last trump" to a series of shofar blasts on the Feast of Trumpets. That is not what was intended.

The word "last" is the Greek word "eschatē" which means "last, final (the furthest, extreme-end)".[77] It is from its root word "eschatos" we derive the word "eschatology", the study of the last things. With the introduction of this "last trump", we find our link to the book of Revelation, just not with the 7th Trumpet judgment. Rather, we find the link in Revelation 4.

Chapter Seven – The Things That Shall Be Hereafter

In Revelation 1, Jesus gave John an outline for the book of Revelation.

> *Revelation 1:19 Write the things which thou hast seen, and the things which are, and the things which shall be hereafter;*[78]

The things which thou "hast seen" refers to the text of Revelation 1. Jesus died on the cross for our sins and rose from the grave in His glorified form. It is in this glorified form He will return at the Second Coming, just as verse 7 says:

> *Revelation 1:7 Behold, he cometh with clouds; and every eye shall see him, and they also which pierced him: and all kindreds of the earth shall wail because of him. Even so, Amen. 8 I am Alpha and Omega, the beginning and the ending, saith the Lord, which is, and which was, and which is to come, the Almighty.*[79]

When John begins to receive his visions from the Lord detailing what he is to write, we are given a necessary piece of information.

> *Revelation 1:10 I was in the Spirit on the Lord's day, and heard behind me a great voice, as of a trumpet,*[80]

The voice as it were of a trumpet was heard on Mount Sinai at the giving of the law. Similarly, the voice of the Trumpet fulfilled the Feast of Trumpets here on earth as the final lawgiver.

> *Hebrews 1:1 God, who at sundry times and in divers manners spake in time past unto the fathers by the prophets, 2 Hath in these last days spoken unto us by his Son, whom he hath appointed heir of all things, by whom also he made the worlds;*[81]

> *Isaiah 33:22 For the L̲ORD̲ is our judge, the L̲ORD̲ is our lawgiver, the L̲ORD̲ is our king; he will save us.[82]*

The voice as it were of the trumpet is also the voice which will give the command to "come up hither". We will see that in just a bit.

Continuing along in Revelation 1, the next instruction Jesus gave John was to write "the things which are". Revelation was written while John was exiled on the island of Patmos in 95 A.D. Jesus died in 32 A.D., thus, John would have been in the church age. "The things which are" include the seven letters to the seven churches contained within Revelation 2-3.

> *Revelation 1:10 I was in the Spirit on the Lord's day, and heard behind me a great voice, as of a trumpet, 11 Saying, I am Alpha and Omega, the first and the last: and, What thou seest, write in a book, and send it unto the seven churches which are in Asia; unto Ephesus, and unto Smyrna, and unto Pergamos, and unto Thyatira, and unto Sardis, and unto Philadelphia, and unto Laodicea.[83]*

In the previous chapter, we discussed the meaning of the "last trump". The sound of the trumpet, which is related to the voice of God, will literally be the last thing to occur within the church age. Thus, we would expect to find another introduction to this trumpet-like voice immediately following the seven letters to the seven churches. Find it, we do.

> *Revelation 4:1 After this I looked, and, behold, a door was opened in heaven: and the first voice which I heard was as it were of a trumpet talking with me; which said, Come up hither, and I will shew thee things which must be hereafter.[84]*

Revelation 4:1 is important for a couple of reasons. First, we have the voice of God telling John to "come up hither" so he can be shown what will occur next. Then, we have the second placement of the word "hereafter" which denotes the beginning of the third section of Revelation, the things which at this point are still entirely prophetic. Not one of them has occurred yet. As we move through Revelation 4, John continues to see more things of import.

> *Revelation 4:2 And immediately I was in the spirit: and, behold, a throne was set in heaven, and one sat on the throne.*

Immediately after receiving the command to "come up hither", John was in the spirit. Why could he not be caught up in flesh and blood? Because flesh and blood cannot inherit the kingdom of God, which at this point is still in heaven. In order to view the events he would need to write about from both an earthly and a heavenly perspective, John needed to be in a form which would allow him to be in the presence of a holy God… because that's what verse 2 tells us he sees immediately: the throne and One who sat on the throne.

There are at least several verses in Revelation 4 and 5 which support the pre-trib rapture of the church. The first has more to do with typology than anything else, and that was found in Revelation 4:1. However, I'm going to do my best to show you how much Revelation 4-5 support the pre-trib rapture, and you'll see it isn't about how things **could** play out but about how they **will** play out. While people interpret things differently, the text only ever supports one conclusion. Stating that chapters 4-5 give us definitive proof of the pre-trib rapture necessitates that we must also be given conclusive proof within the text of Revelation as to when Daniel's 70th Week, or the Tribulation, starts. We are indeed given such proof, and I will get to it in just a bit. For now, we will continue in Revelation 4.

In my opinion, Revelation 4:3 contains one of the most intriguing bit of imagery in the entire book of Revelation.

> *Revelation 4:3 And he that sat was to look upon like a jasper and a sardine stone: and there was a rainbow round about the throne, in sight like unto an emerald.*[85]

Revelation 4:2 told us John saw the throne and He who sits on the throne.

> *1 John 1:5 This then is the message which we have heard of him, and declare unto you, that God is light, and in him is no darkness at all.*[86]

In John 8, Jesus tells us He is the Light of the World. In Matthew 5, we are told we are the light of the world, a city set upon a hill that cannot be hid. I Thessalonians 5 tells us we are all children of light and of the day. Revelation 4:3 shows us the One on the throne is the Father of lights.

> *James 1:17 Every good gift and every perfect gift is from above, and cometh down from the Father of lights, with whom is no variableness, neither shadow of turning.*[87]

He was to look upon like a jasper and a sardine stone. In Exodus 28, we are told what those two stones represent.

> *Exodus 28:15 And thou shalt make the breastplate of judgment with cunning work; after the work of the ephod thou shalt make it; of gold, of blue, and of purple, and of scarlet, and of fine twined linen, shalt thou make it.*
> *16 Foursquare it shall be being doubled; a span shall be the length thereof, and a span shall be the breadth thereof.*
> *17 And thou shalt set in it settings of stones, even four rows of stones: the first row shall be a <u>sardius</u>, a topaz, and a carbuncle: this shall be the first row. 18 And the second row shall be an emerald, a sapphire, and a diamond. 19 And the third row a ligure, an agate, and an amethyst. 20 And the fourth row a beryl, and an onyx, and a <u>jasper</u>: they shall be set in gold in their inclosings. 21 And the stones shall be with the names of the children of Israel, twelve, according to their names, like the engravings of a signet; every one with his name shall they be according to the twelve tribes.*[88]

The jasper and sardine stones represent the first and last stones in the breastplate the high priest wore in the Old Testament, symbolizing the first and last of the twelve tribes of Israel. Thus, the inclusion of the stones in Revelation 4:3 tells us John is beholding the Alpha and

Omega, Yahweh, the God of the first and the last tribe and each tribe in between.

Next, we are told there was a rainbow round about the throne in sight like unto an emerald. The rainbow symbolizes a covenant. In Genesis 9, we are told God put His bow in the sky as a token of His covenant never to destroy the world by water again. Although the Noahic covenant is not in view in Revelation 4, the symbolism shows a covenant is in place. That it surrounds the throne is also important, as it shows the only path to the Father is through this covenant. Furthermore, we are told the rainbow is in sight like unto an emerald. The stones in the breastplate of the high priest included an emerald. It was the fourth stone listed. To ascertain which of the twelve tribes was represented by the emerald, we need to go back to Genesis 29 to see who the fourth son was.

> *Genesis 29:32 And Leah conceived, and bare a son, and she called his name Reuben: for she said, Surely the LORD hath looked upon my affliction; now therefore my husband will love me. 33 And she conceived again, and bare a son; and said, Because the LORD hath heard I was hated, he hath therefore given me this son also: and she called his name Simeon. 34 And she conceived again, and bare a son; and said, Now this time will my husband be joined unto me, because I have born him three sons: therefore was his name called Levi. 35 And she conceived again, and bare a son: and she said, Now will I praise the LORD: therefore she called his name Judah; and left bearing.*[89]

The fourth of the twelve tribes of Israel, the one which was represented by the emerald, was none other than the tribe of Judah. Hebrews 7 explains exactly what is being pictured in Revelation 4:3b.

> *Hebrews 7:11 If therefore perfection were by the Levitical priesthood, (for under it the people received the law,) what further need was there that another priest should rise after the order of Melchisedec, and not be called after the order of Aaron? 12 For the priesthood being changed, there is made*

> *of necessity a change also of the law. 13 For he of whom these things are spoken pertaineth to another tribe, of which no man gave attendance at the altar. 14 For it is evident that our Lord sprang out of Juda; of which tribe Moses spake nothing concerning priesthood. 15 And it is yet far more evident: for that after the similitude of Melchisedec there ariseth another priest, 16 Who is made, not after the law of a carnal commandment, but after the power of an endless life.[90]*

Revelation 4:3 is a picture of God on the throne surrounded by the New Covenant of which Jesus Christ, from the tribe of Judah, is the mediator.

> *I Timothy 2:5 For there is one God, and one mediator between God and men, the man Christ Jesus;[91]*

In Revelation 4:3, we are seeing a word picture which precisely describes Jesus's statement in John 14:6.

> *John 14:6 Jesus saith unto him, I am the way, the truth, and the life: no man cometh unto the Father, but by me.[92]*

Continuing along in Revelation 4, John next sees a group of people. This group provides direct evidence that the rapture will have already occurred by this point.

> *Revelation 4:4 And round about the throne were four and twenty seats: and upon the seats I saw four and twenty elders sitting, clothed in white raiment; and they had on their heads crowns of gold.[93]*

It is the opinion of many prominent Bible scholars the elders are a representation of the whole church. I share their opinion based upon the information we are given concerning the elders. First, we are told they are clothed in white raiment. This clothing denotes them as overcomers by the blood of the Lamb.

> *Revelation 1:5 And from Jesus Christ, who is the faithful witness, and the first begotten of the dead, and the prince of the kings of the earth. Unto him that loved us, and washed us from our sins in his own blood, 6 And hath made us kings and priests unto God and his Father; to him be glory and dominion for ever and ever. Amen.* [94]

> *Revelation 3:5 He that overcometh, the same shall be clothed in white raiment; and I will not blot out his name out of the book of life, but I will confess his name before my Father, and before his angels.* [95]

That the elders are overcomers in Jesus Christ means they are from the church age. How do we know they represent the larger whole and are not simply in heaven in spirit awaiting their resurrection? Because they also have crowns. This tells us the judgment seat of Christ will have already occurred.

> *II Corinthians 5:10 For we must all appear before the judgment seat of Christ; that every one may receive the things done in his body, according to that he hath done, whether it be good or bad.* [96]

In this context, the Greek word for "judgment" is "bema".[97] The following is an excerpt from www.discoverrevelation.com.

> *"The Bema Seat takes its name using imagery from Paul's day. During the ancient Olympics, the judge sat along the finish line. His purpose was not to determine whether or not the participants actually ran the race. If they got that far, then they completed the course. But the Judge at the Bema seat determined how they came in, first, second, and so on, and he handed out the rewards. That is the imagery that the Bible gives us of Believer's Judgment. It is at the Judgment Seat of Life that Christ metes out the rewards not the punishments that we earn in life.*

> *The punishments He has already dealt with by shedding his Blood on the Cross for all those who were willing to trust in*

> *Him. Your rewards are determined according to your works. That is the only place in which your works have any bearing on your eternity. Works won't save you. Only faith in Christ's completed Work on your behalf will. But your works do have a bearing as to your rewards."*[98]

This same principle is discussed by Paul in I Corinthians 3.

> *I Corinthians 3:9 For we are labourers together with God: ye are God's husbandry, ye are God's building. 10 According to the grace of God which is given unto me, as a wise masterbuilder, I have laid the foundation, and another buildeth thereon. But let every man take heed how he buildeth thereupon. 11 For other foundation can no man lay than that is laid, which is Jesus Christ. 12 Now if any man build upon this foundation gold, silver, precious stones, wood, hay, stubble; 13 Every man's work shall be made manifest: for the day shall declare it, because it shall be revealed by fire; and the fire shall try every man's work of what sort it is. 14 If any man's work abide which he hath built thereupon, he shall receive a reward. 15 If any man's work shall be burned, he shall suffer loss: but he himself shall be saved; yet so as by fire.*[99]

The judgment seat of Christ is not about salvation. I Corinthians 3:15 plainly states that regardless of what becomes of our works, "he himself shall be saved". The judgment seat of Christ is where we receive our rewards. Those rewards will come in the form of the crowns mentioned in Revelation 4:4, the very same crowns the elders are later seen casting before the throne in Revelation 4:10. The crowns a believer may earn are as follows:[100]

- The Imperishable Crown – I Corinthians 9:24-25
- The Crown of Rejoicing – I Thessalonians 2:19
- The Crown of Righteousness – II Timothy 4:7-8
- The Crown of Glory – I Peter 5:4
- The Crown of Life – Revelation 2:10

Within two of the crown-related verses above, we are told even more specifically when the crowns will be awarded.

> *I Timothy 4:7 I have fought a good fight, I have finished my course, I have kept the faith: 8 Henceforth there is laid up for me a crown of righteousness, which the Lord, the righteous judge, shall give me at that day: and not to me only, but unto all them also that love his appearing.*[101]

> *I Peter 5:4 And when the chief Shepherd shall appear, ye shall receive a crown of glory that fadeth not away.*[102]

The crowns will be given at the time Jesus appears. They will be given in conjunction with the rapture of the church.

> *II Corinthians 3:18 But we all, with open face beholding as in a glass the glory of the Lord, are changed into the same image from glory to glory, even as by the Spirit of the Lord.*[103]

I Corinthians 3 told us we will be rewarded for good works. Good works are works of faith, works attached to the Spirit. Thus, when this mortal shall put on immortality and this corruptible shall have put on incorruption, all that will be left is that which was of faith and will be for reward. The rest, that which does not stand through the fire, that which is not attached to the Spirit, that which does not stand through the process of being changed from glory to glory, will be burned up.

    If you're like me, you may have wondered why the judgment seat of Christ is never detailed within the book of Revelation. I think the answer is probably very simple. John did not participate in the rapture of the church. He was not changed from glory to glory in order to be in the throne room. He was caught up in the spirit. Thus, he neither witnessed nor participated in the event which will award crowns. He simply saw it had already taken place when he noted the elders already had them.

There is one other verse in Revelation 4 which is relevant to the timing of the rapture of the church.

> *Revelation 4:5 And out of the throne proceeded lightnings and thunderings and voices: and there were seven lamps of fire burning before the throne, which are the seven Spirits of God.*[104]

We have seen God in the throne room. We have seen Jesus in the throne room. We have seen the elders who represent the church in the throne room. Now, we see the Holy Spirit in the throne room. In Revelation 4:2-5, John is seeing physical proof of what was stated in I John 5:7.

> *I John 5:7 For there are three that bear record in heaven, the Father, the Word, and the Holy Ghost: and these three are one.*[105]

The seven Spirits of God is also called the seven-fold Spirit of God. It is not seven different Spirits, but one Spirit with seven attributes.

> *Isaiah 11:1 And there shall come forth a rod out of the stem of Jesse, and a Branch shall grow out of his roots: 2 And the spirit of the LORD shall rest upon him, the spirit of wisdom and understanding, the spirit of counsel and might, the spirit of knowledge and of the fear of the LORD; 3 And shall make him of quick understanding in the fear of the LORD: and he shall not judge after the sight of his eyes, neither reprove after the hearing of his ears: 4 But with righteousness shall he judge the poor, and reprove with equity for the meek of the earth: and he shall smite the earth: with the rod of his mouth, and with the breath of his lips shall he slay the wicked.*[106]

The seven attributes or Spirits of God which are possessed by the Holy Spirit are as follows: wisdom, understanding, counsel, might, knowledge, fear of the Lord, and righteousness. The indwelling nature of these attributes will be removed from earth at the rapture, for a house divided against itself cannot stand.

Lest there be continued disagreement about the timing of the rapture as it relates to the start of Daniel's 70th Week, Revelation 5 also shows us it will be pre-trib.

Chapter Eight – The Seven-Sealed Scroll

In Revelation 4, we were introduced to the elders who represent the church. In Revelation 5, we see them again, this time singing a song about having been redeemed from the earth.

> *Revelation 5:9 And they sung a new song, saying, Thou art worthy to take the book, and to open the seals thereof: for thou wast slain, and hast redeemed us to God by thy blood out of every kindred, and tongue, and people, and nation; 10 And hast made us unto our God kings and priests: and we shall reign on the earth.*[107]

The word "redeemed" is the Greek word "ēgorasas" which comes from the Greek word "agorázō".

> *agorázō* ("acquire by purchasing") stresses *transfer* – i.e. where something becomes *another's belonging* (*possession*). In salvation-contexts, 59 (*agorázō*) is *not* redeeming ("buying back"), but rather focuses on how the believer now *belongs to the Lord as His unique possession* (J. Thayer). Indeed, Christ purchases all the privileges and responsibilities that go with *belonging to Him* (being *in Christ*).[108]

These elders who are singing the song in front of the throne, praising Jesus for being worthy to open the book because He laid His life down for them, are referencing having been raptured, about having reached the day of their redemption.

When we back up to the beginning of the chapter, we see the introduction of a seven-sealed scroll. We will get to what the scroll is in just a bit, but it is important we take note of two things we are shown regarding the scroll: it is currently unopened, and possession of it is being transferred.

> *Revelation 5:1 And I saw in the right hand of him that sat on the throne a book written within and on the backside, sealed*

> with seven seals. 2 And I saw a strong angel proclaiming with a loud voice, Who is worthy to open the book, and to loose the seals thereof? 3 And no man in heaven, nor in earth, neither under the earth, was able to open the book, neither to look thereon. 4 And I wept much, because no man was found worthy to open and to read the book, neither to look thereon. 5 And one of the elders saith unto me, Weep not: behold, the Lion of the tribe of Judah, the Root of David, hath prevailed to open the book, and to loose the seven seals thereof. 6 And I beheld, and, lo, in the midst of the throne and of the four beasts, and in the midst of the elders, stood a Lamb as it had been slain, having seven horns and seven eyes, which are the seven Spirits of God sent forth into all the earth. 7 And he came and took the book out of the right hand of him that sat upon the throne.[109]

That the scroll is yet unopened is significant because of what its opening represents.

> Ezekiel 2:9 And when I looked, behold, an hand was sent unto me; and, lo, a roll of a book was therein; 10 And he spread it before me; and it was written within and without: and there was written therein lamentations, and mourning, and woe.[110]

This idea is similarly described later in Revelation.

> Revelation 10:1 And I saw another mighty angel come down from heaven, clothed with a cloud: and a rainbow was upon his head, and his face was as it were the sun, and his feet as pillars of fire: 2 And he had in his hand a little book open: and he set his right foot upon the sea, and his left foot on the earth, 9 And I went unto the angel, and said unto him, Give me the little book. And he said unto me, Take it, and eat it up; and it shall make thy belly bitter, but it shall be in thy mouth sweet as honey. 10 And I took the little book out of the angel's hand, and ate it up; and it was in my mouth sweet as honey: and as soon as I had eaten it, my belly was bitter.[111]

The scroll was sweet in the mouth, because of what happens at the end. Jesus comes back. It is bitter in the stomach because of the path necessary to get to the end. Judgment.

Revelation 5's unopened scroll implies the judgments have not yet begun. The Seals have not been opened, and the writing within and on the backside of the scroll (Trumpets and Vials) has not been read. It is not until Revelation 6 we see Jesus open the Seals, thus opening the scroll, to begin judging the earth. However, at the beginning of Revelation 5, Jesus does not even have possession of the scroll. Transfer of its possession is shown in Revelation 5:7.

> *Revelation 5:7 And he came and took the book out of the right hand of him that sat upon the throne.*

The transfer of possession from Father to Son is quite significant. As stated, the scroll contains judgments, and we are told in John 5 all judgment has been committed unto the Son.

> *John 5:21 For as the Father raiseth up the dead, and quickeneth them; even so the Son quickeneth whom he will. 22 For the Father judgeth no man, but hath committed all judgment unto the Son:*[112]

Before Jesus begins dispensing wrath and essentially declaring war on unbelief, He will have removed His ambassadors.

> *II Corinthians 5:20 Now then we are ambassadors for Christ, as though God did beseech you by us: we pray you in Christ's stead, be ye reconciled to God.*[113]

The presence of the elders in heaven speaks to this removal. The unopened scroll shows us this removal will be pre-trib. Furthermore, when Jesus rises from His seated position at the right hand of the Father to come get us, the Father will still have possession of it. After bringing the elders (and the rest of church whom the elders represent) to the throne room, Jesus will not resume His seated position. Conversely, John sees Him standing in the throne room. A seated position indicates work has been finished. Jesus sat down at the right hand of the Father after His work was accomplished on the cross and mankind had been redeemed. However, there is more redemptive work to be done. This time, it regards the redemption of the earth, the place where He will return and establish His Kingdom, per the Father's promise.

In the previous chapter, I told you there was definitive proof within the text of Revelation to show us when Daniel's 70th Week starts. If we did not have such proof, Revelation 4 and 5 would be without sufficient context as to define the rapture of the church as pre-trib. Fortunately, we are provided with sufficient context.

> *Revelation 6:1 And I saw when the Lamb opened one of the seals, and I heard, as it were the noise of thunder, one of the four beasts saying, Come and see. 2 And I saw, and behold a white horse: and he that sat on him had a bow; and a crown was given unto him: and he went forth conquering, and to conquer.*[114]

Based on the nature of the scroll containing judgment, and since we can find where the opening of the first Seal occurs and where the pouring out of the last Vial occurs, we can infer beginning and an ending points for Daniel's 70th Week. Revelation 6:1 commences the opening of the seven-sealed scroll. Revelation 16:17 shows us the pouring out of the last Vial.

> *Revelation 16:17 And the seventh angel poured out his vial into the air; and there came a great voice out of the temple of heaven, from the throne, saying, It is done.*[115]

While the Seals, Trumpets, and Vials are individual judgments, they have a singular united purpose. To understand this purpose more fully, it is best to work backwards, from the end to the beginning.

> *Psalm 2:7 I will declare the decree: the LORD hath said unto me, Thou art my Son; this day have I begotten thee. 8 Ask of me, and I shall give thee the heathen for thine inheritance, and the uttermost parts of the earth for thy possession.*

> *9 Thou shalt break them with a rod of iron; thou shalt dash them in pieces like a potter's vessel.*[116]

Verse 9 specifically references the Second Coming, when Jesus will return to defeat those who stand against Him.

> *Revelation 19:11 And I saw heaven opened, and behold a white horse; and he that sat upon him was called Faithful and True, and in righteousness he doth judge and make war. 12 His eyes were as a flame of fire, and on his head were many crowns; and he had a name written, that no man knew, but he himself. 13 And he was clothed with a vesture dipped in blood: and his name is called The Word of God. 14 And the armies which were in heaven followed him upon white horses, clothed in fine linen, white and clean. 15 And out of his mouth goeth a sharp sword, that with it he should smite the nations: and he shall rule them with a rod of iron: and he treadeth the winepress of the fierceness and wrath of Almighty God.*[117]

Why must Jesus defeat all who stand against Him? Psalm 2:8 tells us God has promised a kingdom for Jesus to rule. Said kingdom will encompass the whole of the earth, and the seven-sealed scroll represents the title deed to the earth. From the opening of the first Seal through the pouring out of the seventh Vial, the chapters in Revelation provide the overview of how Jesus will bring a wayward earth under His subjection so He can establish His Millennial Kingdom on it, in total righteousness.

> *Romans 8:18 For I reckon that the sufferings of this present time are not worthy to be compared with the glory which shall be revealed in us. 19 For the earnest expectation of the creature waiteth for the manifestation of the sons of God. 20 For the creature was made subject to vanity, not willingly, but by reason of him who hath subjected the same in hope, 21 Because the creature itself also shall be delivered from the bondage of corruption into the glorious liberty of the children of God. 22 For we know that the whole creation groaneth and travaileth in pain together until now. 23 And*

> *not only they, but ourselves also, which have the firstfruits of the Spirit, even we ourselves groan within ourselves, waiting for the adoption, to wit, the redemption of our body.*[118]

After all the judgments have been accomplished, there will remain nothing more for Jesus to do than return to earth, bringing the Kingdom from heaven with Him. However, approximately seven years before Jesus does so, one will arise who fools the world, and specifically the Jews, into thinking he is their promised Messiah. He will not be.

> *Daniel 9:27 And he shall confirm the covenant with many for one week: and in the midst of the week he shall cause the sacrifice and the oblation to cease, and for the overspreading of abominations he shall make it desolate, even until the consummation, and that determined shall be poured upon the desolate.*[119]

Daniel 9:27 tells us about events which will correspond to three different points during the Week:

- Beginning of the Week – confirmation of the covenant between the Antichrist and Israel's religious leaders
- Middle of the Week – cessation of sacrifices and offerings, Abomination of Desolation
- End of the Week – wrath of God poured upon the "desolator" aka the Antichrist

How does all of that relate to Revelation? When Jesus opens the first Seal in Revelation 6, we are given four pieces of information: there is a rider on a white horse; the rider has a bow; a crown will be given to him; and, he will set off conquering and to conquer.

In Revelation 19, when Jesus returns, He will also be riding a white horse. Revelation 6 is not a reference to Jesus. Rather, it is a reference to the Antichrist. While "anti-" can mean "opposite", it can also mean "one who comes in the place of". Jesus warned the Jews of this very situation in John 5.

> *John 5:43 I am come in my Father's name, and ye receive me not: if another shall come in his own name, him ye will receive.*[120]

Why would the Jews do such a thing? How can they not know the Antichrist is not their true Messiah?

We must bear in mind the indwelling nature of the Holy Spirit will have been removed via the rapture of the church prior to the revelation of the Antichrist. What are the seven attributes of the Spirit? Wisdom, understanding, counsel, might, knowledge, fear of the Lord, and righteousness. Thus, it would seem far simpler for those who do not believe in Jesus to accept one who comes in His place. It doesn't hurt that the Jews are eagerly anticipating the arrival of such a person as we speak. There are those who have contended the rider on the white horse in Revelation 6:2 is Jesus, but we can know for sure that is not the case since Jesus is the one opening the Seal which sets the rider loose.

The second piece of information we are given concerning the opening of the first Seal is that the rider has a bow. While I will address the bow, I would first like to address the other two pieces of information we are given, the next of which tells us this rider has a crown given to him. That a crown is given infers referent power, not legitimate power. The difference between referent power and legitimate power is vast, and noting the difference is extremely important in making the distinction between the Revelation 6:2 crown and the Revelation 19:12 crowns.

Referent power is defined as *"the ability of a leader to influence a follower because of the follower's loyalty, respect, friendship, admiration, affection, or a desire to gain approval"*.[121] The crown denoting this referent power, as given to the rider on the white horse in Revelation 6, is a "stephanos",[122] a victor's crown. However, the crowns Jesus wears in Revelation 19 are not "stephanos". They are diadems. The diadem is a crown fit for a king, no pun intended. Furthermore, the diadem is a symbol of Jesus's legitimate power – power derived from His formal position in the hierarchy of authority.[123]

> *Revelation 19:16 And he hath on his vesture and on his thigh a name written, KING OF KINGS, AND LORD OF LORDS.*[124]

We are also told the rider on the white horse in Revelation 6 sets off conquering and to conquer. The second Seal sees peace being taken from the earth. Peace being removed from the earth stands in direct contrast to the Millennial Kingdom Jesus will establish on earth. His Millennial Kingdom will see no war, whatsoever.

Part of the reason Jesus was rejected by the Jews was because He did not come to deliver them from their bondage, at least not in the way they expected their Messiah would. They wanted a political or military leader who would deliver them from the Roman rule they were under at the time. Jesus came to deliver them from the bondage of their sin, but they were not thinking with an eternal perspective at that time. To their way of thinking, Jesus was of no use to them. However, when the Antichrist comes, the Jews will believe their long-anticipated "deliverer" has arrived. It should be noted, when Jesus returns at the Second Coming, He will do so in exactly that capacity.

> *Joel 3:15 The sun and the moon shall be darkened, and the stars shall withdraw their shining. 16 The LORD also shall roar out of Zion, and utter his voice from Jerusalem; and the heavens and the earth shall shake: but the LORD will be the hope of his people, and the strength of the children of Israel.*[125]

We can now circle back to the bow. It is there we will find our direct link to the start of Daniel's 70th Week.

In Revelation 4:3, John told us of the rainbow he saw roundabout the throne, in sight like unto an emerald. The rainbow shows us a covenant is in place, specifically the New Covenant with the emerald representing Jesus – of the tribe of Judah – as the mediator. Similarly, the bow in Revelation 6:2 also represents a covenant. How can we know this for sure? We were introduced to the bow as the token of a covenant back in Genesis 9.

> *Genesis 9:8 And God spake unto Noah, and to his sons with him, saying, 9 And I, behold, I establish my covenant with you, and with your seed after you; 10 And with every living creature that is with you, of the fowl, of the cattle, and of every beast of the earth with you; from all that go out of the ark, to every beast of the earth. 11 And I will establish my covenant with you, neither shall all flesh be cut off any more by the waters of a flood; neither shall there any more be a flood to destroy the earth. 12 And God said, This is the token of the covenant which I make between me and you and every living creature that is with you, for perpetual generations: 13 I do set my bow in the cloud, and it shall be for a token of a covenant between me and the earth. 14 And it shall come to pass, when I bring a cloud over the earth, that the bow shall be seen in the cloud: 15 And I will remember my covenant, which is between me and you and every living creature of all flesh; and the waters shall no more become a flood to destroy all flesh.*[126]

Today, we call God's bow in the sky a rainbow. However, only the word "bow" is used in the text of Genesis 9. "Bow" is the Hebrew word "qesheth". Its Greek counterpart is the word "tóxon". "Tóxon" is found only once in the New Testament, in Revelation 6:2.[127]

The bow the Revelation 6 rider on the white horse comes with represents a covenant. Thus, per the text of Daniel 9:27 which indicates the 70th Week starts with the confirmation of the covenant, we can pinpoint said start of the week to the opening of the first Seal. As such, we can definitively state the rapture of the church, as noted in Revelation 4 and 5, will be a pre-trib rapture, or more accurately, a pre-70th Week rapture. We are also able to affirm the following:

- The sequence of events laid out in I Thessalonians 4:13-18 – rapture of the church – and I Thessalonians 5:3 – start of the 70th Week upon confirmation of the covenant

The intent of this book has not been to dispute other beliefs about the timing of the rapture. The intent of this book has been to exegete the Biblical text to show how other beliefs about the timing of the rapture are contextually indefensible. Such interpretations would include, but are not limited to, the following:

- Sixth Seal rapture
- Mid-trib rapture
- Pre-wrath rapture
- Post-trib rapture
- No rapture

Chapter Nine – Enoch and Noah

Up to this point, I have stayed away from typology. The Bible is straightforward enough to support the doctrine of the pre-trib rapture without having to use it. However, that isn't to say typologies, or similitudes, do not exist or that they are not useful.

> *Hosea 12:10 I have also spoken by the prophets, and I have multiplied visions, and used similitudes, by the ministry of the prophets.*[128]

While there are more typologies I could choose from, I only want to use two. The first is that of Enoch and Noah. I'm guessing most of you are familiar with the term "the days of Noah". The reference comes from Matthew 24.

> *Matthew 24:37 But as the days of Noah were, so shall also the coming of the Son of man be. 38 For as in the days that were before the flood they were eating and drinking, marrying and giving in marriage, until the day that Noe entered into the ark, 39 And knew not until the flood came, and took them all away; so shall also the coming of the Son of man be.*[129]

To understand the context of those verses, we need to know the age Jesus was in when He spoke those words, as well as who His audience was at the time. Matthew 24 is sandwiched halfway between Matthew 21 and Matthew 27. Matthew 21 describes Jesus's triumphal entry into Jerusalem.

> *Matthew 21:1 And when they drew nigh unto Jerusalem, and were come to Bethphage, unto the mount of Olives, then sent Jesus two disciples, 2 Saying unto them, Go into the village over against you, and straightway ye shall find an ass tied, and a colt with her: loose them, and bring them unto me. 3 And if any man say ought unto you, ye shall say, The Lord hath need of them; and straightway he will send them. 4 All this was done, that it might be fulfilled which was spoken by*

> *the prophet, saying, 5 Tell ye the daughter of Sion, Behold, thy King cometh unto thee, meek, and sitting upon an ass, and a colt the foal of an ass. 6 And the disciples went, and did as Jesus commanded them, 7 And brought the ass, and the colt, and put on them their clothes, and they set him thereon. 8 And a very great multitude spread their garments in the way; others cut down branches from the trees, and strawed them in the way. 9 And the multitudes that went before, and that followed, cried, saying, Hosanna to the son of David: Blessed is he that cometh in the name of the Lord; Hosanna in the highest.[130]*

They might have been welcoming Jesus as the son of David, the "victorious king", but He was coming to them as Isaiah 53's "suffering servant". This coming was prophesied in Zechariah 9, and it was not to deliver them from the Romans. It was to shed His blood for them.

> *Zechariah 9:9 Rejoice greatly, O daughter of Zion; shout, O daughter of Jerusalem: behold, thy King cometh unto thee: he is just, and having salvation; lowly, and riding upon an ass, and upon a colt the foal of an ass. 10 And I will cut off the chariot from Ephraim, and the horse from Jerusalem, and the battle bow shall be cut off: and he shall speak peace unto the heathen: and his dominion shall be from sea even to sea, and from the river even to the ends of the earth. 11 As for thee also, by the blood of thy covenant I have sent forth thy prisoners out of the pit wherein is no water.[131]*

Jesus's triumphal entry into Jerusalem on Nisan 10, four days before Passover, served as the stopping point for the first 69 Weeks of years.

> *Daniel 9:25 Know therefore and understand, that from the going forth of the commandment to restore and to build Jerusalem unto the Messiah the Prince shall be seven weeks, and threescore and two weeks: the street shall be built again, and the wall, even in troublous times. 26 And after threescore and two weeks shall Messiah be cut off, but not for himself:*

and the people of the prince that shall come shall destroy the city and the sanctuary; and the end thereof shall be with a flood, and unto the end of the war desolations are determined.[132]

The command to restore and rebuild Jerusalem came from Artaxerxes on May 14, 445 B.C. Sixty-nine weeks of years takes us to April 6, 32 A.D: Palm Sunday. Between those two dates are 173,880 days.

> 7 Weeks x 7 years per Week x 360 days per year = 17,640 days
>
> 62 Weeks x 7 years per Week x 360 days per year = 156,240 days
>
> 17,640 + 156,240 = 173,880 days

On Nisan 14, four days after His triumphal entry, Jesus went to the cross. The events of His crucifixion are detailed in Matthew 27. Thus, Matthew 24, which contains the Olivet Discourse and Jesus's reference to the "days of Noah", was pre-cross. As a result, they were also pre-New Covenant, pre-church, and pre-rapture. The end of the age and the coming of the Son of man were both references to His Second Coming.

When people liken the times we live in to "the days of Noah", they are unintentionally taking Jesus's words out of context. The days of Noah are not a reference to the church age, nor are they a reference to anything relating to the rapture. Perhaps indirect references can be made, but Noah is not a type of the church or of the rapture. He is a type of Israel, specifically of the remnant, who will be preserved through judgment and come out the other side to "be fruitful and multiply and replenish the earth".

> *Genesis 9:1 And God blessed Noah and his sons, and said unto them, Be fruitful, and multiply, and replenish the earth.*[133]

In the Millennial Kingdom, Israel will do the same.

> *Isaiah 61:9 And their seed shall be known among the Gentiles, and their offspring among the people: all that see them shall acknowledge them, that they are the seed which the LORD hath blessed.*[134]

The typology which rightfully applies to the church and to the rapture is that of Enoch.

> *Hebrews 11:5 By faith Enoch was translated that he should not see death; and was not found, because God had translated him: for before his translation he had this testimony, that he pleased God. 6 But without faith it is impossible to please him: for he that cometh to God must believe that he is, and that he is a rewarder of them that diligently seek him.*[135]

The original story of Enoch and his translation is found in Genesis 5.

> *Genesis 5:18 And Jared lived an hundred sixty and two years, and he begat Enoch: 19 And Jared lived after he begat Enoch eight hundred years, and begat sons and daughters: 20 And all the days of Jared were nine hundred sixty and two years: and he died. 21 And Enoch lived sixty and five years, and begat Methuselah: 22 And Enoch walked with God after he begat Methuselah three hundred years, and begat sons and daughters: 23 And all the days of Enoch were three hundred sixty and five years: 24 And Enoch walked with God: and he was not; for God took him.*[136]

It is interesting to note Enoch was taken from the earth to be with the Lord 669 years before the flood. The symbolism contained within that number equates to the following bullet points and represents everything Enoch was absent for. Thus, it also represents everything the church will be absent for.

- 69 years = 69 Weeks the church was not present for (did not yet exist)

- 600 years = the totality of Noah's life pre-flood
- 7 days = length of time the ark door was open, equating to Daniel's 70th Week
- Door Shut and Flood Starts = Final judgment at the Second Coming

Dr. Chuck Missler composed a fascinating study on the genealogies given in Genesis 5.[137] The names are listed in the generations from Adam to Noah, and Dr. Missler was able to determine the meanings of each name. Together, they foreshadow the Gospel message.

1. Adam - Man
2. Seth – Appointed
3. Enos – Mortal
4. Cainan - Sorrow
5. Mahalaleel – the Blessed God
6. Jared – Shall Come Down
7. **Enoch - Teaching**
8. Methuselah – His Death Shall Bring
9. Lamech – the Despairing
10. **Noah – Comfort or Rest**

As previously stated, Noah represents the remnant of Israel who will be preserved through the final seven years.

> *Joel 2:32 And it shall come to pass, that whosoever shall call on the name of the LORD shall be delivered: for in mount Zion and in Jerusalem shall be deliverance, as the LORD hath said, and in the remnant whom the LORD shall call.*[138]

The remnant will enter the Lord's rest, otherwise known as His Millennial Kingdom. However, the story is a little different with Enoch. Enoch was entirely removed from anything having to do with Noah. In fact, Enoch was not on earth for any part of Noah's life. Furthermore, Enoch's name means "teaching". What commission were believers given?

> *Matthew 28:19 Go ye therefore, and **teach** all nations, baptizing them in the name of the Father, and of the Son, and of the Holy Ghost: 20 **Teaching** them to observe all things whatsoever I have commanded you: and, lo, I am with you always, even unto the end of the world. Amen.*[139]

When we get to Genesis 7, we see the link between Noah and the remnant of Israel more clearly delineated.

> *Genesis 7:1 And the LORD said unto Noah, Come thou and all thy house into the ark; for thee have I seen righteous before me in this generation. 2 Of every clean beast thou shalt take to thee by sevens, the male and his female: and of beasts that are not clean by two, the male and his female. 3 Of fowls also of the air by sevens, the male and the female; to keep seed alive upon the face of all the earth. 4 For yet seven days, and I will cause it to rain upon the earth forty days and forty nights; and every living substance that I have made will I destroy from off the face of the earth. 5 And Noah did according unto all that the LORD commanded him. 6 And Noah was six hundred years old when the flood of waters was upon the earth. 7 And Noah went in, and his sons, and his wife, and his sons' wives with him, into the ark, because of the waters of the flood. 8 Of clean beasts, and of beasts that are not clean, and of fowls, and of every thing that creepeth upon the earth, 9 There went in two and two unto Noah into the ark, the male and the female, as God had commanded Noah. 10 And it came to pass after seven days, that the waters of the flood were upon the earth.*

After all the animals were gathered in, and after Noah and his family entered, the door to the ark remained open for seven days. This seven days equates to the seven years of Daniel's 70th Week. Anyone who chooses to enter in through the open door will be saved from the final judgment reserved for the Second Coming of Jesus.

> *II Peter 3:7 But the heavens and the earth, which are now, by the same word are kept in store, reserved unto fire against the day of judgment and perdition of ungodly men.*[140]

However, they must enter the ark before the door is shut.

> *Genesis 7:16 And they that went in, went in male and female of all flesh, as God had commanded him: and the LORD shut him in. 17 And the flood was forty days upon the earth; and the waters increased, and bare up the ark, and it was lift up above the earth. 18 And the waters prevailed, and were increased greatly upon the earth; and the ark went upon the face of the waters. 19 And the waters prevailed exceedingly upon the earth; and all the high hills, that were under the whole heaven, were covered. 20 Fifteen cubits upward did the waters prevail; and the mountains were covered. 21 And all flesh died that moved upon the earth, both of fowl, and of cattle, and of beast, and of every creeping thing that creepeth upon the earth, and every man: 22 All in whose nostrils was the breath of life, of all that was in the dry land, died.[141]*

Only Noah and his family were faithful. Similarly, faith during the 70th Week will be hard to come by.

> *Micah 7:1 Woe is me! for I am as when they have gathered the summer fruits, as the grapegleanings of the vintage: there is no cluster to eat: my soul desired the firstripe fruit. 2 The good man is perished out of the earth: and there is none upright among men: they all lie in wait for blood; they hunt every man his brother with a net. 3 That they may do evil with both hands earnestly, the prince asketh, and the judge asketh for a reward; and the great man, he uttereth his mischievous desire: so they wrap it up. 4 The best of them is as a brier: the most upright is sharper than a thorn hedge: the day of thy watchmen and thy visitation cometh; now shall be their perplexity. 5 Trust ye not in a friend, put ye not confidence in a guide: keep the doors of thy mouth from her that lieth in thy bosom. 6 For the son dishonoureth the father, the daughter riseth up against her mother, the daughter in law against her mother in law; a man's enemies are the men of his own house. 7 Therefore I will look unto the LORD; I will wait for the God of my salvation: my God will hear me.[142]*

The door people must enter through is Jesus Christ. Although they might lose their earthly life, only Jesus can save their eternal life. There is, however, a limited time in which people must make their choice. Tomorrow is never guaranteed, let alone being able to survive the entire seven years of hell on earth. Once He returns at the Second Coming, the door will be closed and there will be no more option for boarding the ark.

> *John 10:1 Verily, verily, I say unto you, He that entereth not by the door into the sheepfold, but climbeth up some other way, the same is a thief and a robber. 2 But he that entereth in by the door is the shepherd of the sheep. 3 To him the porter openeth; and the sheep hear his voice: and he calleth his own sheep by name, and leadeth them out. 4 And when he putteth forth his own sheep, he goeth before them, and the sheep follow him: for they know his voice. 5 And a stranger will they not follow, but will flee from him: for they know not the voice of strangers. 6 This parable spake Jesus unto them: but they understood not what things they were which he spake unto them. 7 Then said Jesus unto them again, Verily, verily, I say unto you, I am the door of the sheep. 8 All that ever came before me are thieves and robbers: but the sheep did not hear them. 9 I am the door: by me if any man enter in, he shall be saved, and shall go in and out, and find pasture. 10 The thief cometh not, but for to steal, and to kill, and to destroy: I am come that they might have life, and that they might have it more abundantly.*[143]

> *John 14:6 Jesus saith unto him, I am the way, the truth, and the life: no man cometh unto the Father, but by me.*[144]

So, are we in the days of Noah? No, we are not. Thankfully, we never will be. Fortunately for us, we have a loving God who has promised to take us out of harm's way. Like Enoch, we walk with God and will not be, for God will take us.

Chapter Ten – The Ancient Jewish Wedding Ceremony

The second typology, or similitude, I want to use applies to that of the Jewish wedding.

Ephesians 4 and 5 provide symbolism for Jesus and the church in two capacities. In Ephesians 4, the church is compared to a body. This body is fitly joined together, with Christ as the head. Just as with a human body, the head is responsible for directing the overall function of each part to achieve a unified objective.

> *Ephesians 4:11 And he gave some, apostles; and some, prophets; and some, evangelists; and some, pastors and teachers; 12 For the perfecting of the saints, for the work of the ministry, for the edifying of the body of Christ: 13 Till we all come in the unity of the faith, and of the knowledge of the Son of God, unto a perfect man, unto the measure of the stature of the fulness of Christ: 14 That we henceforth be no more children, tossed to and fro, and carried about with every wind of doctrine, by the sleight of men, and cunning craftiness, whereby they lie in wait to deceive; 15 But speaking the truth in love, may grow up into him in all things, which is the head, even Christ: 16 From whom the whole body fitly joined together and compacted by that which every joint supplieth, according to the effectual working in the measure of every part, maketh increase of the body unto the edifying of itself in love.*[145]

The imagery provided in Ephesians 4 is taken a step further in Ephesians 5 where the singular body represents the cleaving together of two persons, a husband and wife. However, the message being given is not only about an earthly husband and wife relationship. Its context is about Jesus and the church.

> *Ephesians 5:22 Wives, submit yourselves unto your own husbands, as unto the Lord. 23 For the husband is the head of the wife, even as Christ is the head of the church: and he is the saviour of the body. 24 Therefore as the church is subject*

> *unto Christ, so let the wives be to their own husbands in every thing. 25 Husbands, love your wives, even as Christ also loved the church, and gave himself for it; 26 That he might sanctify and cleanse it with the washing of water by the word, 27 That he might present it to himself a glorious church, not having spot, or wrinkle, or any such thing; but that it should be holy and without blemish. 28 So ought men to love their wives as their own bodies. He that loveth his wife loveth himself. 29 For no man ever yet hated his own flesh; but nourisheth and cherisheth it, even as the Lord the church: 30 For we are members of his body, of his flesh, and of his bones. 31 For this cause shall a man leave his father and mother, and shall be joined unto his wife, and they two shall be one flesh. 32 This is a great mystery: but I speak concerning Christ and the church.*[146]

To this point, no marriage between Jesus and the church has taken place. Paul tells us in II Corinthians 11 we are still in the betrothal stage.

> *II Corinthians 11:2 For I am jealous over you with godly jealousy: for I have espoused you to one husband, that I may present you as a chaste virgin to Christ.*[147]

We have been promised to Jesus, but the fulfillment of the promise is yet forward looking. John gives us even more information about the relationship between Jesus and the church in John 3.

> *John 3:27 John answered and said, A man can receive nothing, except it be given him from heaven. 28 Ye yourselves bear me witness, that I said, I am not the Christ, but that I am sent before him. 29 He that hath the bride is the bridegroom: but the friend of the bridegroom, which standeth and heareth him, rejoiceth greatly because of the bridegroom's voice: this my joy therefore is fulfilled.*[148]

John alludes to Jesus as the bridegroom and those who are in Christ as the bride. This knowledge was, as John stated, revealed to him from heaven since the church did not yet exist. How do we know when the wedding between Jesus and the church will take place? The answer to that question is found within the Jewish wedding typology.

The Jewish wedding involves three groups of people: the bridegroom, the bride, and the wedding guests. We have already discussed Jesus and the church as respective bridegroom and bride. We will discuss who the guests are in greater detail as we work our way through each facet of the wedding. The following is an excerpt taken from www.bridalcovenant.com.

> *"What does Scripture mean when it refers to the church as a bride and Jesus as a bridegroom? Is this just flowery language? Is it merely indicating God's love for His people? Understanding ancient Jewish wedding practices makes the meaning of Scripture clear. The wedding is a picture of the covenant Jesus made and reveals His plans to return for His bride, the church. The people of ancient Israel understood what Jesus was going to do because they understood the model of the wedding. The analogy between a wedding and Christ and the Church is described in Ephesians 5:31-32, "For this reason a man will leave his father and mother and be united to his wife, and the two will become one flesh." This is a profound mystery -- but I am talking about Christ and the church." The following overviews the practices of an ancient Jewish betrothal and wedding. In parallel, it shows how Jesus has fulfilled the betrothal portion of the wedding and how He may fulfill the remainder when He comes again for His bride, the church."*[149]

In addition to the three groups of people, there are also three dominant aspects of the Jewish wedding: the betrothal, which is the stage we are currently in; the wedding ceremony; and, the wedding feast. There are nine steps to the whole of the Jewish wedding, six of which belong to the betrothal stage. We will begin by taking a walk through each of them. During our walk, we will also see how Jesus has fulfilled each step.

The Marriage Covenant and the Bride Price

"When a young man desired to marry a young woman in ancient Israel, he would prepare a contract or covenant to present to the young woman and her father at the young woman's home. The contract showed his willingness to provide for the young woman and described the terms under which he would propose marriage. The most important part of the contract was the bride price, the price that the young man was willing to pay to marry the young woman. This payment was to be made to the young woman's father in exchange for his permission to marry. The bride price was generally quite high. Sons were considered to be more valuable than daughters since they were physically more able to share in the work of farming and other heavy labor. The bride price compensated the young woman's family for the cost to raise a daughter and also indicated the love that the young man had for the young woman -- the young woman was very valuable to the young man! The young man would go to the young woman's house with the contract and present his offer to the young woman and her father."[150]

How has Jesus fulfilled this step?

"Jesus came to the home of His bride (Earth) to present His marriage contract. The marriage contract provided by Jesus is the new covenant, which provides for the forgiveness of sins of God's people. Jesus paid the bride price with His life. At the last supper, when breaking bread, He spoke of the price He was paying: "...This is my body given for you..." Luke 22:20. In Hebrews 8:15 it makes clear that Jesus died as the price for the new covenant: "...Christ is the mediator of a new covenant, that those who are called may receive the promised eternal inheritance -- now that he has died as a ransom to set them free from the sins committed under the first covenant. Other Scripture references include 1 Corinthians 6:19-20, 1 Peter 1:18-19, Acts 20:28 and John 3:29."[151]

The letter to the church of the Laodiceans contains this same imagery. The Laodiceans were the only church of the seven listed in Revelation 2-3 which had no believers in it.

> *Revelation 3:20 Behold, I stand at the door, and knock: if any man hear my voice, and open the door, I will come in to him, and will sup with him, and he with me.*[152]

In this verse, we see Jesus coming to the home of the desired bride wishing to offer the marriage covenant which is also the New Covenant. All one must do is open the door and invite Him in, accepting the covenant He desires to make with them. The bride price has already been paid.

The Cup

"If the bride price was agreeable to the young woman's father, the young man would pour a glass of wine for the young woman. If the young woman drank the wine, it would indicate her acceptance of the proposal. At this point, the young man and young woman would be betrothed. Betrothal was legally binding, just like a marriage. The only difference was that the marriage was not yet consummated. A typical betrothal period was 1-2 years. During this time the bride and bridegroom each would be preparing for the marriage and wouldn't see each other."[153]

How has Jesus fulfilled this step?

"Just as the bridegroom would pour a cup of wine for the bride to drink to seal the marriage contract, so Jesus poured wine for His disciples. His words described the significance of the cup in representing the bride price for the marriage contract: Then He took the cup, gave thanks and offered it to them, saying, "Drink from it, all of you. This is my blood of the covenant, which is poured out for many for the forgiveness of sins. I tell you, I will not drink of this fruit of the vine from now on until that day when I drink it anew with you in my Father's kingdom." The disciples drank of the cup, thus accepting the contract. Matthew 26:28-29"[154]

The disciples represented the earliest members of the church. When each of us accepts Jesus as our Savior, we also accept the token of the New Covenant – the cup which symbolizes His shed blood on the cross for the remission of our sins. His death on the cross was the first of three components to the Gospel message.

I Corinthians 15:1 Moreover, brethren, I declare unto you the gospel which I preached unto you, which also ye have received, and wherein ye stand; 2 By which also ye are saved, if ye keep in memory what I preached unto you, unless ye have believed in vain. 3 For I delivered unto you first of all that which I also received, how that Christ died for our sins according to the scriptures; 4 And that he was buried, and that he rose again the third day according to the scriptures:[155]

Hebrews 9 explains the concept of the cup and its representation of the shedding of blood in conjunction with the offering of the New Covenant.

Hebrews 9:16 For where a testament is, there must also of necessity be the death of the testator. 17 For a testament is of force after men are dead: otherwise it is of no strength at all while the testator liveth.

Hebrews 9:22 And almost all things are by the law purged with blood; and without shedding of blood is no remission. 23 It was therefore necessary that the patterns of things in the heavens should be purified with these; but the heavenly things themselves with better sacrifices than these. 24 For Christ is not entered into the holy places made with hands, which are the figures of the true; but into heaven itself, now to appear in the presence of God for us: 25 Nor yet that he should offer himself often, as the high priest entereth into the holy place every year with blood of others; 26 For then must he often have suffered since the foundation of the world: but now once in the end of the world hath he appeared to put away sin by the sacrifice of himself.[156]

As a side note, I thought it was interesting that the amount of time the groom spent away from his betrothed was 1-2 years. This correlates, in thousands of years, to the length of time our betrothed has been away from us.

Gifts for the Bride

"Next, the bridegroom would present the bride with special gifts. The purpose of these gifts was to show the bridegroom's appreciation of the bride. They were also intended to help her to remember him during the long betrothal period."[157]

How has Jesus fulfilled this step?

"The gifts that Jesus gave us are the gifts of the Holy Spirit: We know that we live in Him and He in us, because He has given us of His Spirit 1 John 4:13. Jesus described this gift in John 14:26: But the Counselor, the Holy Spirit, whom the Father will send in my name, will teach you all things and will remind you of everything I have said to you. Peace I leave with you; my peace I give you. I do not give to you as the world gives. Do not let your hearts be troubled and do not be afraid."[158]

Jesus sent the Comforter on Pentecost, a gift which indwells each of us who are in Christ and seals us from the day of our justification unto the day of our glorification.

Ephesians 1:11 In whom also we have obtained an inheritance, being predestinated according to the purpose of him who worketh all things after the counsel of his own will: 12 That we should be to the praise of his glory, who first trusted in Christ. 13 In whom ye also trusted, after that ye heard the word of truth, the gospel of your salvation: in whom also after that ye believed, ye were sealed with that holy Spirit of promise, 14 Which is the earnest of our inheritance until the redemption of the purchased possession, unto the praise of his glory.[159]

Ephesians 4:30 And grieve not the holy Spirit of God, whereby ye are sealed unto the day of redemption.[160]

Mikveh

> *"The bride would next partake of a Mikveh, or cleansing bath. Mikveh is the same word used for baptism. To this day in conservative Judaism a bride cannot marry without a Mikveh."[161]*

How has Jesus fulfilled this step?

> *"The Mikveh, or baptism that Jesus provided for His bride was baptism in the Holy Spirit. On one occasion, while He was eating with them, He gave them this command: "Do not leave Jerusalem, but wait for the gift my Father promised, which you have heard me speak about. For John baptized with water, but in a few days you will be baptized with the Holy Spirit." Acts 1:4"[162]*

Indeed, on the day of Pentecost, those who were gathered in Jesus's name received the baptism of the Holy Spirit.

> *Acts 2:1 And when the day of Pentecost was fully come, they were all with one accord in one place. 2 And suddenly there came a sound from heaven as of a rushing mighty wind, and it filled all the house where they were sitting. 3 And there appeared unto them cloven tongues like as of fire, and it sat upon each of them. 4 And they were all filled with the Holy Ghost, and began to speak with other tongues, as the Spirit gave them utterance.[163]*

Each of us receives the baptism of the Holy Spirit immediately upon belief in Jesus Christ.

> *"The baptism of the Holy Spirit may be defined as that work whereby the Spirit of God places the believer into union with Christ and into union with other believers in the body of Christ at the moment of salvation."[164]*

Preparing a Place

> *"During the betrothal period, the bridegroom would prepare a wedding chamber for the honeymoon. This chamber was typically built in the bridegroom's father's house or on his father's property. The wedding chamber had to be a beautiful place to bring the bride. The bride and groom were to spend __seven days__ there. The wedding chamber had to be built to the groom's father's specifications. The young man could go for his bride only when his father approved."*[165]

How has Jesus fulfilled this step?

> *"Just as a bridegroom would have told his bride that he would go to prepare a place for her, so Jesus told His disciples: "...In my Father's house are many rooms or mansions; if it were not so, I would have told you. I am going there to prepare a place for you. And if I go and prepare a place for you, I will come back and take you to be with me that you also may be where I am. John 14:1-3"*[166]

In the above text, I underlined a point of interest – seven days spent in the wedding chamber. We will come to understand the relevance of that time as we work our way through the remaining steps of the Jewish wedding. In the interim, we now come to the final step of the betrothal aspect. This final step is a bit different since the onus is not on the bridegroom, but on the bride.

A Waiting Bride Consecrated

> *"While the bridegroom was preparing the wedding chamber, the bride was considered to be consecrated, set apart or "bought with a price". If she went out, she would wear a veil so others would know she was betrothed. During this time she prepared herself for the marriage. She likely had saved money all her life for this time. She would purchase expensive cosmetics and learn to apply them to make herself more beautiful for the bridegroom. She wouldn't know when her groom would come for her, so she always had to be ready."*[167]

How is this being fulfilled?

> *"We, God's people, are now consecrated, or set apart, waiting for the return of our bridegroom at The Rapture. We should be spending this time preparing ourselves for Jesus' return."*[168]

This final stage of the betrothal process is all about the process of "present sanctification". The overall process of sanctification is three-fold and includes past sanctification, present sanctification, and perfective sanctification. These three stages are what we also refer to as justification, sanctification, and glorification. Partaking of the cup symbolizes our acceptance of and entrance into the New Covenant, and it is what we call our justification. Once we have been justified, we begin the process of sanctification which is more commonly referred to as our walk with the Lord. While we are alive on this earth, we work on our relationships with our Savior, learning more about Him and leading others to Him. We strive for unity within the body of Christ, furthering the Gospel message and, hopefully, longing for the day our bridegroom comes to retrieve us.

The day the bridegroom comes for his bride is the next step of the Jewish wedding. It represents movement from the betrothal aspect to the wedding aspect. It represents the movement from present to prophetic. It also represents our perfective sanctification, or glorification.

Bridegroom Comes for His Bride

> *"When the bridegroom's father deemed the wedding chamber ready, the father would tell the bridegroom that all was ready and to get His bride. The bridegroom would abduct his bride secretly... and take her to the wedding chamber. As the bridegroom approached the bride's home, he would shout and blow the shofar (ram's horn trumpet)..."* [169]

How will this be fulfilled?

> *"Just as the bridegroom would come for the bride in the middle of the night, with a shout and the sound of a shofar, so the Lord will come for us. For the Lord himself will come down from heaven, with a loud command, with the voice of the archangel and with the trumpet call of God, and the dead in Christ will rise first. After that, we who are still alive and are left will be caught up together with them in the clouds to meet the Lord in the air. And so we will be with the Lord forever. Therefore encourage each other with these words. 1 Thessalonians 4:16-17"* [170]

The coming of the Bridegroom for the bride is the rapture of the church. This is the day Jesus will appear, having brought all those who died in Christ with Him. Their earthly bodies will be resurrected, and we who are alive will be caught up with them to meet our Lord in the air. He will then take us to the place He has prepared for us, His Father's house, which is heaven.

Seven Days in the Wedding Chamber

"The bridegroom would take his bride to the wedding chamber where they would spend seven days. The bridegroom's friend would wait outside the door of the wedding chamber. When the marriage was consummated, the bridegroom would tell his friend through the door, and the friend would announce it to the assembled guests. The guests would celebrate for seven days until the bride and bridegroom emerged from the wedding chamber. At this time the groom would bring his wife out and introduce her to the community."[171]

How will this be fulfilled?

"Ancient Jewish eschatology taught that a seven year "time of trouble" would come upon the earth before the coming of the Messiah. During that time of trouble, the righteous would be resurrected and would enter the wedding chamber where they would be protected from the time of trouble. Today that seven year period is referred to, by Christians, as the Tribulation, and as Birth Pangs by the Jews. After 7 years in Heaven the Groom, Christ, will bring His wife to Earth and at the time of His Second Coming He will introduce her to the community on Earth."[172]

Here, we find a very specific link to the pre-trib rapture of the church. The bride will be snatched from the earth and taken to heaven to spend the whole of Daniel's 70th Week away from the events on earth. This time in heaven represents the fulfillment of Jesus's promise in Revelation 3.

Revelation 3:10 Because thou hast kept the word of my patience, I also will keep thee from the hour of temptation, which shall come upon all the world, to try them that dwell upon the earth.[173]

There is a segment within the Bible prophecy community who believes the pre-trib rapture of the church could come a period of years before the start of Daniel's 70th Week. From the typology of the Jewish wedding, we observe that cannot be the case. There is no Scriptural basis for such a gap between the rapture and the start of Daniel's 70th Week. Furthermore, the bride will spend only seven days in the wedding chamber. This seven days in the wedding chamber correlates perfectly to the seven years of Daniel's 70th Week.

After the marriage and time spent in the wedding chamber, it will be time for the wedding feast, also called the marriage supper. The marriage supper is the final aspect of the Jewish wedding.

Marriage Supper

"After seven days in the wedding chamber, the bride and bridegroom would emerge and participate in a feast with friends and family. There would be joyous celebrating during this feast. The feast would conclude the wedding celebration."[174]

How will this be fulfilled?

"As the bride and bridegroom celebrated with a joyous wedding supper, so Jesus and His bride, the church will celebrate the marriage. Then I heard what sounded like a great multitude, like the roar of rushing waters and like loud peals of thunder, shouting: "Hallelujah! For our Lord God Almighty reigns. Let us rejoice and be glad and give him glory! For the wedding of the Lamb has come, and his bride has made herself ready. Fine linen, bright and clean, was given her to wear." (Fine linen stands for the righteous acts of the saints) Then the angel said to me, "Write: 'Blessed are those who are invited to the wedding supper of the Lamb!'". Revelation 19:6-9"

There are differing thoughts regarding the timing of the marriage supper of the Lamb and where it will occur. However, many prominent Bible scholars agree the marriage supper of the Lamb will take place on earth immediately following the Second Coming of Jesus Christ. This can be observed in Matthew 25 and Luke 12.

Matthew 25:1 Then shall the kingdom of heaven be likened unto ten virgins, which took their lamps, and went forth to meet the bridegroom. 2 And five of them were wise, and five were foolish. 3 They that were foolish took their lamps, and took no oil with them: 4 But the wise took oil in their vessels with their lamps. 5 While the bridegroom tarried, they all slumbered and slept. 6 And at midnight there was a cry made, Behold, the bridegroom cometh; go ye out to meet him. 7 Then all those virgins arose, and trimmed their lamps.

> *8 And the foolish said unto the wise, Give us of your oil; for our lamps are gone out. 9 But the wise answered, saying, Not so; lest there be not enough for us and you: but go ye rather to them that sell, and buy for yourselves. 10 And while they went to buy, the bridegroom came; and they that were ready went in with him to the marriage: and the door was shut. 11 Afterward came also the other virgins, saying, Lord, Lord, open to us. 12 But he answered and said, Verily I say unto you, I know you not. 13 Watch therefore, for ye know neither the day nor the hour wherein the Son of man cometh.*[175]

The day and hour wherein the Son of man cometh is a reference to the Second Coming. Many people inaccurately interpret the parable of the 10 virgins as having to do with the church and with the rapture. However, the text above shows the bridegroom arriving and entering the location he has arrived at. He does not retrieve a bride and take her to his father's house. This parable is representative of the marriage supper, not the marriage. The wise virgins do not represent the bride. They represent the guests who will go into the marriage supper with the bridegroom and his bride who will be with him. Luke 12 affirms this.

> *Luke 12:35 Let your loins be girded about, and your lights burning; 36 And ye yourselves like unto men that wait for their lord, when he will return from the wedding; that when he cometh and knocketh, they may open unto him immediately. 37 Blessed are those servants, whom the lord when he cometh shall find watching: verily I say unto you, that he shall gird himself, and make them to sit down to meat, and will come forth and serve them.*[176]

Those who are bid entry into the marriage supper of the Lamb are also being bid entry into His Millennial Kingdom. It is for this reason Revelation 19 refers to those who are called to the marriage supper of the Lamb as "blessed". At this point, the Jewish wedding will have reached its conclusion.

From all we have just gone through, it should be clear to see only a pre-trib rapture will fit the typology of the Jewish wedding.

Chapter Eleven – The Jewish Wedding and the First Adam

For those who may be leery of accepting the Jewish wedding typology for the pre-trib rapture of the church, I decided to add something I had not previously planned on writing. It is also something I had not considered prior to a few days ago. In I Corinthians 15, Jesus is referred to as the second Adam.

> *I Corinthians 15:47 The first man is of the earth, earthy; the second man is the Lord from heaven.*
>
> *I Corinthians 15:21 For since by man came death, by man came also the resurrection of the dead. 22 For as in Adam all die, even so in Christ shall all be made alive.*[177]

There is a larger issue at play within the Jewish wedding typology than simply linking it to the rapture of the church. Regarding Jesus and the church, the Jewish wedding typology represents the restoration of a relationship between God and man which has been lost from the Garden of Eden. When we go back to the Garden, we can identify that the steps of the Jewish wedding were also present in the covenant God made with man. The Jewish wedding typology as it relates to God and Adam is essentially the reverse of the typology between Christ and the church. The first moved from perfection to separation. The second moves from separation to perfection. We just saw at the latter. Now, we will look at the former.

The Marriage Covenant and the Bride Price

Dispensations begin with covenants, and from his creation to his expulsion, man's time in the Garden of Eden was no exception. In the Garden, the dispensation was called "the age of innocence". Our present dispensation is called the "age of grace" or "the church age".

Ephesians 5, which talks about the husband/wife relationship between Christ and the church, quotes text taken directly from Genesis 2. However, the covenant which existed in the Garden of Eden was between God and Adam. The covenant was made, the age of innocence begotten, when God created man in His own image.

> *Genesis 1:26 And God said, Let us make man in our image, after our likeness: and let them have dominion over the fish of the sea, and over the fowl of the air, and over the cattle, and over all the earth, and over every creeping thing that creepeth upon the earth. 27 So God created man in his own image, in the image of God created he him; male and female created he them.*[178]

> *Genesis 2:7 And the LORD God formed man of the dust of the ground, and breathed into his nostrils the breath of life; and man became a living soul.*[179]

With respect to Jesus and the church, the New Covenant was designed to bring lost people into relationship with God. However, in the Garden of Eden, immediately after He was created, man already had a perfect relationship with God.

The Cup

In the New Covenant, the cup symbolizes the shedding of Jesus's blood for the remission of sins. However, in the Garden, no sin existed. Therefore, the application of the cup is not what man needed to do to bridge a gap. Rather, it was what man needed to do to keep a gap from existing.

> *Genesis 2:16 And the L<small>ORD</small> God commanded the man, saying, Of every tree of the garden thou mayest freely eat: 17 But of the tree of the knowledge of good and evil, thou shalt not eat of it: for in the day that thou eatest thereof thou shalt surely die.*[180]

Gifts for the Bride

After man's creation, what did God give him as gifts? For starters, He gave woman to man.

> *Genesis 2:18 And the LORD God said, It is not good that the man should be alone; I will make him an help meet for him. 19 And out of the ground the LORD God formed every beast of the field, and every fowl of the air; and brought them unto Adam to see what he would call them: and whatsoever Adam called every living creature, that was the name thereof. 20 And Adam gave names to all cattle, and to the fowl of the air, and to every beast of the field; but for Adam there was not found an help meet for him. 21 And the LORD God caused a deep sleep to fall upon Adam, and he slept: and he took one of his ribs, and closed up the flesh instead thereof; 22 And the rib, which the LORD God had taken from man, made he a woman, and brought her unto the man. 23 And Adam said, This is now bone of my bones, and flesh of my flesh: she shall be called Woman, because she was taken out of Man. 24 Therefore shall a man leave his father and his mother, and shall cleave unto his wife: and they shall be one flesh.*[181]

Then He gave man and woman dominion over the whole of creation.

> *Genesis 1:28 And God blessed them, and God said unto them, Be fruitful, and multiply, and replenish the earth, and subdue it: and have dominion over the fish of the sea, and over the fowl of the air, and over every living thing that moveth upon the earth. 29 And God said, Behold, I have given you every herb bearing seed, which is upon the face of all the earth, and every tree, in the which is the fruit of a tree yielding seed; to you it shall be for meat. 30 And to every beast of the earth, and to every fowl of the air, and to every thing that creepeth upon the earth, wherein there is life, I have given every green herb for meat: and it was so. 31 And God saw every thing that he had made, and, behold, it was*

very good. And the evening and the morning were the sixth day.[182]

Mikveh

In the Jewish wedding typology between Jesus and the church, the mikveh was represented by the baptism of the Holy Spirit. However, in Eden, man was given God's Spirit right from the very beginning.

> *Genesis 2:7 And the LORD God formed man of the dust of the ground, and breathed into his nostrils the breath of life; and man became a living soul.[183]*

Just as Jesus was conceived of the Holy Ghost, Adam was also God's direct creation. In the above verse, "breath" is the same word for "spirit". Thus, the Spirit breathed into Adam was that of the Holy Spirit. In I Corinthians 15:45, we are told the following:

> *I Corinthians 15:45 And so it is written, The first man Adam was made a living soul; the last Adam was made a quickening spirit.[184]*

God's Spirit within Adam gave Adam life. God's Spirit within Jesus gave Jesus the ability to give life.

Preparing a Place

This step of the Jewish wedding typology is probably pretty easy to figure out.

> *Genesis 2:8 And the L*ORD *God planted a garden eastward in Eden; and there he put the man whom he had formed.*[185]

The Waiting Bride Consecrated

In the previous chapter, "the waiting bride consecrated" was all about what the bride did while the groom was away, in preparation for his return. What did Adam do while God was away? Unfortunately, nothing good.

> *Genesis 3:6 And when the woman saw that the tree was good for food, and that it was pleasant to the eyes, and a tree to be desired to make one wise, she took of the fruit thereof, and did eat, and gave also unto her husband with her; and he did eat. 7 And the eyes of them both were opened, and they knew that they were naked; and they sewed fig leaves together, and made themselves aprons.*[186]

Thus, the age of innocence came to an abrupt end. Their eyes were opened, and they were naked and ashamed. This is how the unbelieving world will appear when Jesus returns at the Second Coming.

> *Revelation 16:15 Behold, I come as a thief. Blessed is he that watcheth, and keepeth his garments, lest he walk naked, and they see his shame.*[187]

And how the Laodiceans currently appear, those to whom Jesus is knocking on the door and attempting to offer the marriage covenant to.

> *Revelation 3:17 Because thou sayest, I am rich, and increased with goods, and have need of nothing; and knowest not that thou art wretched, and miserable, and poor, and blind, and naked: 18 I counsel thee to buy of me gold tried in the fire, that thou mayest be rich; and white raiment, that thou mayest be clothed, and that the shame of thy nakedness do not appear; and anoint thine eyes with eyesalve, that thou mayest see.*[188]

"The waiting bride consecrated" in the Jewish wedding typology as it relates to God and Adam represents the fall of man.

Bridegroom Comes for His Bride

Then God came for Adam…

> *Genesis 3:8 And they heard the voice of the* L<small>ORD</small> *God walking in the garden in the cool of the day: and Adam and his wife hid themselves from the presence of the* L<small>ORD</small> *God amongst the trees of the garden. 9 And the* L<small>ORD</small> *God called unto Adam, and said unto him, Where art thou? 10 And he said, I heard thy voice in the garden, and I was afraid, because I was naked; and I hid myself.*[189]

Seven Days in the Wedding Chamber

Do we know how long Adam and Eve were in the Garden of Eden? Not for sure, no. However, there are a few ideas regarding the subject. I have not conducted the research myself, but I was told by a few different people the extra-Biblical texts of Jasher and Jubilees place Adam and Eve in the Garden for seven years. If correct, the typology would be the same as the number of years the church spends in heaven with Jesus after the rapture. However, I do not believe seven years is accurate in this case. I believe the amount of time Adam and Eve spent in the Garden of Eden prior to being removed from it was none other than seven days. The following excerpt was taken from www.biblescienceguy.com and gives a good interpretation of why their time in the Garden had to be so short.

> *Scripture does not explicitly say how long after Creation the Fall occurred. Based on some Scriptural hints, I think it happened soon — within a week to a month.*
> *Jesus seems to hint that the Fall occurred near the Beginning when He described Satan as* "a murderer from the beginning" *(John 8:44). The serpent's lie to Eve resulted in death to Adam and Eve and death to all their descendants, certainly qualifying Satan as the murderer Jesus says he was* "from the beginning."
>
> *Adam was 130 at Seth's birth which followed Cain's murder of Abel. The population had to be fairly large at that time because Cain worried about people killing him as he wandered the earth. No children were born before the Fall, so the Fall must have been close to Creation in order to produce a significant population from multiple generations in at most 130 years. (Genesis 5:3; 4:25; 4:1-15)*
>
> *A more particular indication of how long Adam was in Eden may be deduced from Eve's timeline. Eve was the first wife and mother, created to be Adam's companion and helper and to bear his children. Her first child Cain was conceived after expulsion from Eden (Genesis 4:1). Before the Fall, the*

> *human reproductive system would be working perfectly, and Adam and Eve would be in complete harmony. God had commanded them to be fruitful and multiply and fill the earth (Genesis 1:28). Prior to the Fall, they would have been obedient to this first command from Yahweh. Their physically perfect bodies could have conceived in the first reproductive cycle.*
>
> *Why didn't Eve conceive in the Garden of Eden? I think it was because Adam and Eve must not have stayed in Eden long enough to reach the fertile portion of a reproductive cycle. Provided the cycle was the same length before the Fall as after the Fall, they were probably expelled from Eden within two weeks, at most a month, after Creation. They may have only been in the Garden of Eden for a few days.*
>
> *Satan, who tempted Eve to sin, must have rebelled and fallen from his state of perfection after Yahweh pronounced all of Creation "very good" on Day Six (Genesis 1:31) and before Adam's fall not long thereafter.*[190]

Assuming Creation began on Tishri 1, God created for six days and rested on the seventh. If we assume the "seven days in the wedding chamber" typology is accurate, we would be taken to Tishri 14. Although the first month was not changed from Tishri to Abib until Exodus, the symbolism of the fourteenth day of the first month certainly applies in this case. How so? Because of what was done to cover the sins of Adam and Eve prior to their expulsion from the Garden.

> *Genesis 3:21 Unto Adam also and to his wife did the LORD God make coats of skins, and clothed them.*[191]

The first Passover sacrifice. It is for this reason Jesus is called the Lamb slain from the foundation of the world.

Lastly, we come to the end of the Jewish wedding typology with the marriage supper.

Marriage Supper

In Revelation 19, those who are invited to the marriage supper of the Lamb are called "blessed". Furthermore, Luke 12 tells us they will sit down to eat and be served. The opposite is true in both cases regarding the typology in Eden. Adam was cursed, and he would have to get his own food.

> *Genesis 3:17 And unto Adam he said, Because thou hast hearkened unto the voice of thy wife, and hast eaten of the tree, of which I commanded thee, saying, Thou shalt not eat of it: cursed is the ground for thy sake; in sorrow shalt thou eat of it all the days of thy life; 18 Thorns also and thistles shall it bring forth to thee; and thou shalt eat the herb of the field; 19 In the sweat of thy face shalt thou eat bread, till thou return unto the ground; for out of it wast thou taken: for dust thou art, and unto dust shalt thou return.*

And although there were no guests yet for them to join once they left the wedding chamber, they were still required to leave.

> *Genesis 3:22 And the LORD God said, Behold, the man is become as one of us, to know good and evil: and now, lest he put forth his hand, and take also of the tree of life, and eat, and live for ever: 23 Therefore the LORD God sent him forth from the garden of Eden, to till the ground from whence he was taken. 24 So he drove out the man; and he placed at the east of the garden of Eden Cherubims, and a flaming sword which turned every way, to keep the way of the tree of life.*[192]

Chapter Twelve – The Divisiveness of the Pre-Trib Rapture

The biggest reason I wanted to include the Jewish wedding typology as it related to Adam was because of what happens when we don't listen to God. While there are none of us who understand everything in the Bible with absolute clarity, nor is there any one of us who has everything right, the Word of God does provide all the answers we need. The very first sin was committed because Satan deceived Eve into questioning the validity of the word of God. And how long did it take for Adam and Eve to fall after they had been created? Seven days. That's it. Just a mere seven days.

When we are told Jesus will establish His Millennial Kingdom in righteousness, we are also told Satan will be bound for that entire time and without the ability to deceive the nations.

> *Revelation 20:3 And cast him into the bottomless pit, and shut him up, and set a seal upon him, that he should deceive the nations no more, till the thousand years should be fulfilled: and after that he must be loosed a little season.*[193]

Perhaps we can understand a little more about why Satan's binding is necessary. If Satan deceived one perfect being, I don't even want to consider what implications that might have if he were not bound during Christ's Millennial Reign. More to the point, even in their perfection, and even when they had direct access to God, it only took seven days for Satan to mess things up. And what will he do once again, immediately after he is released?

> *Revelation 20:7 And when the thousand years are expired, Satan shall be loosed out of his prison, 8 And shall go out to deceive the nations which are in the four quarters of the earth, Gog, and Magog, to gather them together to battle: the number of whom is as the sand of the sea.*[194]

He will immediately return to the activity he was deprived of for those 1000 years.

We are not perfect. We are not sinless. But we are sinners saved by the grace of a loving God. Satan cannot make someone fall who is already fallen, but he can cause division. The pre-trib rapture is one of the most divisive topics within the church today. Why? Because there is a crown associated to it.

> *II Timothy 4:7-8 I have fought a good fight, I have finished my course, I have kept the faith: 8 Henceforth there is laid up for me a crown of righteousness, which the Lord, the righteous judge, shall give me at that day: and not to me only, but unto all them also that love his appearing.*

What did Jesus tell us to do?

> *Revelation 3:11 Behold, I come quickly: hold that fast which thou hast, that no man take thy crown.*[195]

We should always keep in mind that whenever there is a battle within the church, it is always of a spiritual nature.

> *Ephesians 6:10 Finally, my brethren, be strong in the Lord, and in the power of his might. 11 Put on the whole armour of God, that ye may be able to stand against the wiles of the devil. 12 For we wrestle not against flesh and blood, but against principalities, against powers, against the rulers of the darkness of this world, against spiritual wickedness in high places. 13 Wherefore take unto you the whole armour of God, that ye may be able to withstand in the evil day, and having done all, to stand.*[196]

Sometimes the battles come from intentional misleading. Sometimes the battles come from lack of knowledge. Sometimes the battles come from misunderstanding or misinterpretation. There are those who have difficulty distinguishing between the rapture of the church and the Second Coming of Jesus Christ. While illuminating the differences between the two events did not previously have a place within the scope of this book, I found it pertinent to include at this point. It is extremely important for us to be able to distinguish between the two.

The chart below contains some of the most notable differences between the rapture of the church and the Second Coming of Jesus Christ. These and others can be found at www.pre-trib.org. They were compiled by Dr. Thomas Ice in an article entitled <u>Differences Between the Rapture and the Second Coming</u>.[197]

Rapture of the Church	Second Coming of Jesus Christ
Translation/changing of all believers	No translation at all
Translated saints go to heaven	Translated saints return to earth
Earth not judged	Earth judged & righteousnes established
Imminent, signless	Follows definite predicted signs, including Tribulation
Not in the Old Testament	Predicted often in the Old Testament
Believers only	Affects all men
Before the day of wrath	Concludes the day of wrath
No reference to Satan	Satan bound
Christ comes *for* His own	Christ comes *with* His own
Jesus comes in the *air*	Jesus comes to *earth*
Jesus comes to claim His bride	Jesus comes with His bride
Only His own will see Jesus	Every eye will see Jesus
Tribulation begins	Millennial Kingdom begins

Thank you all for taking the time to read about the pre-trib rapture of the church. This is one of my favorite topics to discuss, not because I want to escape this world or because life is just too hard. Not even close! This is one of my favorite topics, because I long for the day I can see my Jesus face-to-face and begin my eternity with Him. This is my blessed hope. I "hope" it is yours, too. May God bless you all.

> *Proverbs 3:5 Trust in the LORD with all thine heart; and lean not unto thine own understanding. 6 In all thy ways acknowledge him, and he shall direct thy paths.*[198]

About the Author

Heather lives in Michigan with her son and her cat. She has a Master's degree in Management from Walsh College and is currently employed as an analyst. When not working, she can usually be found at home researching Bible prophecy or with her nose stuck in a book. Heather has a YouTube channel which she uses to teach Bible prophecy. She also conducts routine Bible studies using the "chapter-by-chapter, verse-by verse" methodology. Her YouTube channel is named "Heather R", and she hopes you will stop by and visit sometime.

This is Heather's fourth self-published work.

References

[1] https://www.biblegateway.com/passage/?search=Genesis+1&version=KJV
[2] https://www.biblegateway.com/passage/?search=Genesis+2&version=KJV
[3] https://www.biblegateway.com/passage/?search=hebrews+10&version=KJV
[4] https://www.biblegateway.com/passage/?search=hebrews+2&version=KJV
[5] https://www.biblegateway.com/passage/?search=john+1&version=KJV
[6] http://biblehub.com/hebrew/5397.htm
[7] https://www.biblegateway.com/passage/?search=I+Corinthians+2&version=KJV
[8] https://www.biblegateway.com/passage/?search=John+4%3A24&version=KJV
[9] https://www.biblegateway.com/passage/?search=hebrews+10&version=KJV
[10] https://www.biblegateway.com/passage/?search=john+10&version=KJV
[11] https://www.biblegateway.com/passage/?search=II+Corinthians+5&version=KJV
[12] https://www.biblegateway.com/passage/?search=isaiah+53&version=KJV
[13] https://www.biblegateway.com/passage/?search=I+Corinthians+15&version=KJV
[14] https://www.biblegateway.com/passage/?search=John+2&version=KJV
[15] https://www.biblegateway.com/passage/?search=matthew+12&version=KJV
[16] https://www.biblegateway.com/passage/?search=Matthew+26&version=KJV
[17] https://www.biblegateway.com/passage/?search=Matthew+27&version=KJV
[18] https://www.biblegateway.com/passage/?search=john+10&version=KJV
[19] https://www.biblegateway.com/passage/?search=matthew+28&version=KJV
[20] https://www.biblegateway.com/passage/?search=I+Corinthians+15&version=KJV
[21] https://www.biblegateway.com/passage/?search=revelation+1&version=KJV
[22] https://www.biblegateway.com/passage/?search=I+Corinthians+15&version=KJV
[23] https://www.biblegateway.com/passage/?search=I+Corinthians+15&version=KJV
[24] https://www.biblegateway.com/passage/?search=Revelation+20&version=KJV
[25] https://www.biblegateway.com/passage/?search=John+6&version=KJV
[26] https://www.biblegateway.com/passage/?search=John+5&version=KJV
[27] https://www.biblegateway.com/passage/?search=matthew+13&version=KJV
[28] https://www.biblegateway.com/passage/?search=matthew+24&version=KJV
[29] https://www.biblegateway.com/passage/?search=Hosea+6&version=KJV
[30] https://www.biblegateway.com/passage/?search=Daniel+12&version=KJV
[31] https://www.biblegateway.com/passage/?search=Matthew+24&version=KJV
[32] https://www.biblegateway.com/passage/?search=Matthew+27&version=KJV
[33] https://www.biblegateway.com/passage/?search=revelation+20&version=KJV
[34] https://www.biblegateway.com/passage/?search=Hebrews+8&version=KJV
[35] https://www.biblegateway.com/passage/?search=Hebrews+10&version=KJV
[36] https://www.biblegateway.com/passage/?search=Hebrews+2&version=KJV
[37] https://www.biblegateway.com/passage/?search=Matthew+27&version=KJV
[38] https://www.biblegateway.com/passage/?search=Romans+11&version=KJV

[39] https://www.biblegateway.com/passage/?search=acts+15&version=KJV
[40] https://www.biblegateway.com/passage/?search=Ephesians+3&version=KJV
[41] https://www.biblegateway.com/passage/?search=galatians+3&version=KJV
[42] https://www.biblegateway.com/passage/?search=Romans+11&version=KJV
[43] https://www.biblegateway.com/passage/?search=Romans+10&version=KJV
[44] https://www.biblegateway.com/passage/?search=john+3&version=KJV
[45] https://www.biblegateway.com/passage/?search=Ephesians+2&version=KJV
[46] https://www.biblegateway.com/passage/?search=colossians+2&version=KJV
[47] https://www.biblegateway.com/passage/?search=Hebrews+9&version=KJV
[48] https://www.biblegateway.com/passage/?search=Matthew+26&version=KJV
[49] https://www.biblegateway.com/passage/?search=I+Thessalonians+5&version=KJV
[50] https://www.biblegateway.com/passage/?search=Ezekiel+39&version=KJV
[51] https://www.biblegateway.com/passage/?search=Daniel+9&version=KJV
[52] https://www.biblegateway.com/passage/?search=Romans+11&version=KJV
[53] https://www.biblegateway.com/passage/?search=john+16&version=KJV
[54] https://www.biblegateway.com/passage/?search=john+15&version=KJV
[55] http://biblehub.com/greek/2347.htm
[56] https://www.biblegateway.com/passage/?search=Revelation+3&version=KJV
[57] http://biblehub.com/greek/3986.htm
[58] https://www.biblegateway.com/passage/?search=II+Peter+3&version=KJV
[59] https://www.biblegateway.com/passage/?search=Hebrews+10&version=KJV
[60] https://www.biblegateway.com/passage/?search=john+5&version=KJV
[61] https://www.biblegateway.com/passage/?search=Romans+5&version=KJV
[62] http://biblehub.com/greek/1997.htm
[63] https://www.biblegateway.com/passage/?search=II+Thessalonians+2&version=KJV
[64] https://www.biblegateway.com/passage/?search=1%20Thessalonians+3&version=KJV
[65] https://www.biblegateway.com/passage/?search=zechariah+14&version=KJV
[66] https://www.biblegateway.com/passage/?search=1%20Thessalonians+4&version=KJV
[67] https://www.biblegateway.com/passage/?search=1+Thessalonians+5&version=KJV
[68] https://www.biblegateway.com/passage/?search=II+Peter+3%3A10&version=KJV
[69] https://www.biblegateway.com/passage/?search=Revelation+16&version=KJV
[70] https://www.biblegateway.com/passage/?search=Revelation+3&version=KJV
[71] https://www.biblegateway.com/passage/?search=Daniel+9&version=KJV
[72] https://www.biblegateway.com/passage/?search=I+Corinthians+15&version=KJV

73 https://www.biblegateway.com/passage/?search=II+Corinthians+5&version=KJV
74 https://www.biblegateway.com/passage/?search=I+Corinthians+15&version=KJV
75 https://www.biblegateway.com/passage/?search=John+14&version=KJV
76 https://www.biblegateway.com/passage/?search=Exodus+19&version=KJV
77 http://biblehub.com/greek/2078.htm
78 https://www.biblegateway.com/passage/?search=revelation+1&version=KJV
79 https://www.biblegateway.com/passage/?search=revelation+1&version=KJV
80 https://www.biblegateway.com/passage/?search=revelation+1&version=KJV
81 https://www.biblegateway.com/passage/?search=Hebrews+1&version=KJV
82 https://www.biblegateway.com/passage/?search=Isaiah+33&version=KJV
83 https://www.biblegateway.com/passage/?search=revelation+1&version=KJV
84 https://www.biblegateway.com/passage/?search=revelation+4&version=KJV
85 https://www.biblegateway.com/passage/?search=revelation+4&version=KJV
86 https://www.biblegateway.com/passage/?search=I+john+1&version=KJV
87 https://www.biblegateway.com/quicksearch/?quicksearch=father+of+lights.&qs_version=KJV
88 https://www.biblegateway.com/passage/?search=Exodus+28&version=KJV
89 https://www.biblegateway.com/passage/?search=Genesis+29&version=KJV
90 https://www.biblegateway.com/passage/?search=Hebrews+7&version=KJV
91 https://www.biblegateway.com/passage/?search=1%20Timothy+2&version=KJV
92 https://www.biblegateway.com/passage/?search=John+14&version=KJV
93 https://www.biblegateway.com/passage/?search=Revelation+4&version=KJV
94 https://www.biblegateway.com/passage/?search=Revelation+1&version=KJV
95 https://www.biblegateway.com/passage/?search=Revelation+3&version=KJV
96 https://www.biblegateway.com/passage/?search=II+Corinthians+5&version=KJV
97 http://biblehub.com/lexicon/2_corinthians/5-10.htm
98 http://www.discoverrevelation.com/10.html
99 https://www.biblegateway.com/passage/?search=I+Corinthians+3&version=KJV
100 https://www.gotquestions.org/heavenly-crowns.html
101 https://www.biblegateway.com/passage/?search=II+Timothy+4&version=KJV
102 https://www.biblegateway.com/passage/?search=I+Peter+5&version=KJV
103 https://www.biblegateway.com/passage/?search=II+Corinthians+3&version=KJV
104 https://www.biblegateway.com/passage/?search=Revelation+4&version=KJV
105 https://www.biblegateway.com/passage/?search=I+John+5%3A7&version=KJV
106 https://www.biblegateway.com/passage/?search=Isaiah+11&version=KJV
107 https://www.biblegateway.com/passage/?search=Revelation+5&version=KJV
108 http://biblehub.com/greek/59.htm
109 https://www.biblegateway.com/passage/?search=Revelation+5&version=KJV

110 https://www.biblegateway.com/passage/?search=Ezekiel+2&version=KJV
111 https://www.biblegateway.com/passage/?search=Revelation+10&version=KJV
112 https://www.biblegateway.com/passage/?search=John+5&version=KJV
113 https://www.biblegateway.com/quicksearch/?quicksearch=Ambassadors&qs_version=KJV
114 https://www.biblegateway.com/passage/?search=Revelation+6&version=KJV
115 https://www.biblegateway.com/passage/?search=revelation+16&version=KJV
116 https://www.biblegateway.com/passage/?search=Psalm+2&version=KJV
117 https://www.biblegateway.com/passage/?search=revelation+19&version=KJV
118 https://www.biblegateway.com/passage/?search=Romans+8&version=KJV
119 https://www.biblegateway.com/passage/?search=Daniel+9&version=KJV
120 https://www.biblegateway.com/passage/?search=John+5&version=KJV
121 https://en.wikipedia.org/wiki/Referent_power
122 http://biblehub.com/greek/4735.htm
123 http://study.com/academy/lesson/legitimate-power-in-leadership-definition-example-quiz.html
124 https://www.biblegateway.com/passage/?search=revelation+19&version=KJV
125 https://www.biblegateway.com/passage/?search=Joel+3&version=KJV
126 https://www.biblegateway.com/passage/?search=Genesis+9&version=KJV
127 http://www.studylight.org/desk/interlinear.cgi?search_form_type=interlinear&q1=Genesis+9%3A13&ot=lxx&nt=wh&s=0&t3=str_nas&ns=0
128 https://www.biblegateway.com/quicksearch/?quicksearch=similitude&qs_version=KJV
129 https://www.biblegateway.com/passage/?search=Matthew+24&version=KJV
130 https://www.biblegateway.com/passage/?search=Matthew+21&version=KJV
131 https://www.biblegateway.com/passage/?search=zechariah+9&version=KJV
132 https://www.biblegateway.com/passage/?search=Daniel+9&version=KJV
133 https://www.biblegateway.com/passage/?search=genesis+9&version=KJV
134 https://www.biblegateway.com/passage/?search=Isaiah+61%3A9&version=KJV
135 https://www.biblegateway.com/passage/?search=Hebrews+11&version=KJV
136 https://www.biblegateway.com/passage/?search=Genesis+5&version=KJV
137 http://www.khouse.org/articles/1996/44/
138 https://www.biblegateway.com/passage/?search=Joel+2&version=KJV
139 https://www.biblegateway.com/passage/?search=Matthew+28&version=KJV
140 https://www.biblegateway.com/passage/?search=II+Peter+3&version=KJV
141 https://www.biblegateway.com/passage/?search=Genesis+7&version=KJV
142 https://www.biblegateway.com/passage/?search=micah+7&version=KJV
143 https://www.biblegateway.com/passage/?search=John+10&version=KJV
144 https://www.biblegateway.com/passage/?search=John+14&version=KJV
145 https://www.biblegateway.com/passage/?search=Ephesians+4&version=KJV
146 https://www.biblegateway.com/passage/?search=ephesians+5&version=KJV

147 https://www.biblegateway.com/passage/?search=II+Corinthians+11&version=KJV
148 https://www.biblegateway.com/passage/?search=John+3&version=KJV
149 http://www.bridalcovenant.com/wedding1.html
150 http://www.bridalcovenant.com/wedding1.html
151 http://www.bridalcovenant.com/wedding1.html
152 https://www.biblegateway.com/passage/?search=Revelation+3&version=KJV
153 http://www.bridalcovenant.com/wedding1.html
154 http://www.bridalcovenant.com/wedding1.html
155 https://www.biblegateway.com/passage/?search=I+Corinthians+15&version=KJV
156 https://www.biblegateway.com/passage/?search=Hebrews+9&version=KJV
157 http://www.bridalcovenant.com/wedding1.html
158 http://www.bridalcovenant.com/wedding1.html
159 https://www.biblegateway.com/passage/?search=Ephesians+1&version=KJV
160 https://www.biblegateway.com/passage/?search=Ephesians+4&version=KJV
161 http://www.bridalcovenant.com/wedding1.html
162 http://www.bridalcovenant.com/wedding1.html
163 https://www.biblegateway.com/passage/?search=Acts+2&version=KJV
164 https://www.gotquestions.org/Spirit-baptism.html
165 http://www.bridalcovenant.com/wedding1.html
166 http://www.bridalcovenant.com/wedding1.html
167 http://www.bridalcovenant.com/wedding1.html
168 http://www.bridalcovenant.com/wedding1.html
169 http://www.bridalcovenant.com/wedding1.html
170 http://www.bridalcovenant.com/wedding1.html
171 http://www.bridalcovenant.com/wedding1.html
172 http://www.bridalcovenant.com/wedding1.html
173 https://www.biblegateway.com/passage/?search=Revelation+3&version=KJV
174 http://www.bridalcovenant.com/wedding1.html
175 https://www.biblegateway.com/passage/?search=Matthew+25&version=KJV
176 https://www.biblegateway.com/passage/?search=Luke+12&version=KJV
177 https://www.biblegateway.com/passage/?search=I+Corinthians+15&version=KJV
178 https://www.biblegateway.com/passage/?search=Genesis+1&version=KJV
179 https://www.biblegateway.com/passage/?search=Genesis+2&version=KJV
180 https://www.biblegateway.com/passage/?search=Genesis+2&version=KJV
181 https://www.biblegateway.com/passage/?search=Genesis+2&version=KJV
182 https://www.biblegateway.com/passage/?search=Genesis+1&version=KJV
183 https://www.biblegateway.com/passage/?search=Genesis+2&version=KJV
184 https://www.biblegateway.com/passage/?search=I+Corinthians+15&version=KJV
185 http://raptureintheairnow.com/?topic=first-adam-last-adam-the-ancient-jewish-wedding
186 https://www.biblegateway.com/passage/?search=Genesis+3&version=KJV

[187] https://www.biblegateway.com/passage/?search=Revelation+16%3A15&version=KJV

[188] https://www.biblegateway.com/passage/?search=Revelation+3&version=KJV

[189] https://www.biblegateway.com/passage/?search=Genesis+3&version=KJV

[190] https://biblescienceguy.wordpress.com/2015/12/09/how-long-was-adam-in-eden/

[191] https://www.biblegateway.com/passage/?search=Genesis+3&version=KJV

[192] https://www.biblegateway.com/passage/?search=Genesis+3&version=KJV

[193] https://www.biblegateway.com/passage/?search=Revelation+20&version=KJV

[194] https://www.biblegateway.com/passage/?search=Revelation+20&version=KJV

[195] https://www.biblegateway.com/passage/?search=Revelation+3&version=KJV

[196] https://www.biblegateway.com/passage/?search=Ephesians+6&version=KJV

[197] http://www.pre-trib.org/articles/view/differences-between-rapture-and-second-coming

[198] https://www.biblegateway.com/passage/?search=Proverbs+3&version=KJV

Printed in Great Britain
by Amazon